Lisa Maria Martin

EVERYDAY INFORMATION ARCHITECTURE

D1722281

MORE FROM A BOOK APART

Progressive Web Apps
Jason Grigsby

Flexible Typesetting
Tim Brown

Going Offline
Jeremy Keith

Conversational Design
Erika Hall

The New CSS Layout
Rachel Andrew

Accessibility for Everyone
Laura Kalbag

Practical Design Discovery
Dan Brown

Demystifying Public Speaking
Lara Hogan

JavaScript for Web Designers
Mat Marquis

Practical SVG
Chris Coyier

Visit abookapart.com for our full list of titles.

Publisher: Jeffrey Zeldman
Designer: Jason Santa Maria
Executive Director: Katel LeDû
Managing Editor: Lisa Maria Martin
Editor: Katel LeDû
Reviewer: Donna Lichaw
Copyeditor: Mary van Ogtrop
Proofreader: Katel LeDû
Book Producer: Ron Bilodeau

ISBN: 978-1-937557-74-4

A Book Apart
New York, New York
http://abookapart.com

TABLE OF CONTENTS

1   *Introduction*

4

CHAPTER 1
Systems of Organization

18

CHAPTER 2
Content Analysis

36

CHAPTER 3
Categories and Labels

56

CHAPTER 4
Site Structure

75

CHAPTER 5
Navigation and Wayfinding

99

CHAPTER 6
Tags and Taxonomies

116   *Conclusion*

117   *Acknowledgments*

119   *Resources*

122   *References*

125   *Index*

For Mat.

FOREWORD

I LIKE TO THINK OF MYSELF as an organized person. A tangled mess of assorted cables? Sorted into Ziploc bags. Gift wrap and ribbon? That's why the Container Store exists. Books and music? Don't even question it, lest I spend thirty minutes boring you with a discussion of my own personal metadata management system.

At least, I used to be an organized person, back when I lived in a 500-square-foot apartment. A couple years ago, I moved to a house three times that size, with a basement. As my possessions drifted across four floors of a row house, I discovered something unpleasant about myself: I hadn't been organized. I'd been constrained. I'd only been able to find things easily because there were so few places where things could *be*. In my new home, I struggled to define a system that accommodated new spaces: the guest bathroom, the office closet, the basement cupboard. My identity as an organized person went missing—just like my hammer.

"Why did they put that *there*?" is the question of our age. We've all experienced the web as bewildered users at one time or another, clicking around a confusing navigation bar, or searching for something we *know* exists behind a mystifying label. Much like my new house, the web lacks constraints that make content easy to find, label, and organize. With an infinite number of pages in your bandwidth, you can put your content anywhere. No wonder nobody can find anything.

If you're staring down your own web content organization project, this book will be your guide. While you may feel daunted by the prospect of making sense of all the pages and topics and content and ideas and tumbleweeds that have collected on your website over the years, Lisa Maria will walk you through the process of organizing it. When you're done, you won't have to wonder if your content makes sense to the people it's there to serve.

I wonder if she knows where my hammer is?

—Karen McGrane

INTRODUCTION

WALTER PLECKER WAS AN ASSHOLE.

In the 1920s, he was registrar of Virginia's Bureau of Vital Statistics, the state government office that controlled birth, death, marriage, and divorce records (http://bkaprt.com/eia/00-01/). As a frothing-at-the-mouth white supremacist, Plecker was terrified of interracial marriage. Its very existence, he insisted, was the result of poor categorization: white people were marrying non-white people only because the government hadn't labeled them "correctly."

Plecker decided that he could use bureaucracy to change this, and he was right: all he had to do was relabel Virginia's racial categories, and racist laws took care of the rest. He reduced the number of racial identity categories to just two, then altered and enforced documentation to reflect his definitions.

This meant that a very small and specific group of people were labeled *white*, and everyone who fell outside of Plecker's narrow view were *not*—and their lives changed accordingly. The government saw them differently, identified them differently, treated them differently. They no longer had access to the same public spaces, the same schools, the same services and safety nets afforded to white people. Marriages were invalidated. Children were separated from parents. Virginians lost agency over who they were—all because Walter Plecker changed a label.

Changing a label is a *design* decision—one calculated, in this case, to disenfranchise specific human beings.

Now, most of us don't have Walter Plecker's job. We are, instead, designers, developers, copywriters, strategists. We work on the web, and we may not think our work carries that same weight.

I'm here to argue that it does. Whatever our role, we are designers of information. Our choices alter the presentation and flow of human knowledge. We control how people find, understand, and use information in every facet of their lives.

We must be very, very careful.

Our work, our responsibility

"The creative organization of information creates new information," wrote architect Richard Saul Wurman. This axiom is at the core of our work. When we organize information—that is, when we structure it, order it, display it, label it, connect it—we alter it. We change how information will be perceived, for better or for worse.

That's a lot of power—power that we don't always recognize is ours. And when we don't recognize it, we can't be careful about its impact. We risk building sites that aren't clear, usable, or inclusive. We risk alienating, even harming, users.

And users have enough cards stacked against them already. Information literacy is low, stress is high, distractions are abundant, and capitalism is a grind. Everyone—users and web workers alike—is trying to navigate an internet that is both mandatory and hostile, that craves our data but cares little for how it makes us feel.

As builders of the web, we have a responsibility to change that. And we can—by being more communicative, more ethical, and more empowering in our organizational choices.

The goal of this book is to help you do just that. You may not consider yourself an information architect, but maybe you've been tasked with assessing and categorizing your site's content. Or you've just jumped in on an unfamiliar sitemap project. Or you've never built a taxonomy before. Wherever you're coming from, the principles and practices of information architecture can help you craft more thoughtful information spaces.

Our journey won't be exhaustive when it comes to information architecture, but we will look at the everyday work of the web through a structural lens. In Chapter 1, we'll discuss the importance of organizational frameworks. In Chapter 2, we'll learn how content can inform strategy and scope. Chapter 3 examines the building blocks of sitemaps, while Chapter 4 shows us how to put them together. In Chapter 5, we'll ensure that users can find their way, while Chapter 6 explores the applications (and implications) of taxonomies.

All the while, we'll be thinking about why we're doing this at all: to help people find, understand, and use information—information that can make a difference in their lives. Because if we aren't going to use our power for good, who will?

Three, two, one, let's jam.

1

SYSTEMS OF ORGANIZATION

You can alphabetize [books] by author. You can divide them by genre. You can group all the paperbacks together. You can reserve a shelf for autographed books or first editions. Then there are less sensible but still reasonable ways to organize your books. You can shelve them by size. You can shelve them chronologically. You can shelve them by category: books you've read, books you haven't read, books you probably will never read. You can even (shudder) shelve them by the color of the book jackets. [...Books displayed spine-in] clearly are not books, but props.
—LAURIE HERTZEL (http://bkaprt.com/eia/01-01/)

WHEN WE ORGANIZE INFORMATION, we change it. The order in which it appears, the content that precedes or follows it, the ways we expand or condense it—everything we do to arrange information will alter its meaning.

The key is to alter it in a way that enhances understanding. Organization is structure, and structure "make[s] every subject easier to understand and remember," wrote Barbara Ann Kipfer in *The Order of Things*. "[It] can speed access to related information [and] make sense of our detailed, complex world."

In other words: well-organized information is easier for humans to grok than poorly organized information. And as long as the organization of information is the result of design decisions, well, therein lies our responsibility—lest we end up with information that is structured but doesn't serve users (like books with their spines turned inward).

LATCH: A FRAMEWORK

When we begin to organize information on a website, it can feel like a subjective exercise. How are you supposed to know how to approach seemingly arbitrary collections of content, especially when that content has multiple owners, each with their own emphatic opinions about the best place to put it on the site? (The homepage. It's always the homepage.)

To avoid this sense of crushing arbitrariness, we need a *framework*—some structure to help us *create* structure.

Don't think for a moment that the organizational problems we encounter online are by any means new! Humans have a rich and storied history of organizational systems—memory palaces, Linnaean taxonomy, the periodic table of elements, the Dewey Decimal system, *heck*, index cards (this list goes on, but it's been gently suggested that I rein in my, uh, enthusiasm). What all of these systems have in common is just that: they are *systems*. They are frameworks. They all offer rules for structuring the content that falls under their purview.

There are many useful frameworks we can explore to understand the principles of organization, but let's look closely at one developed by architect Richard Saul Wurman. "While information may be infinite," he wrote, "the ways of structuring it are not." When we're experiencing information overload, that's a really powerful idea. Structure puts sensible organization well within our reach!

Wurman proposed that there are five possible methods—yes, *just five!*—for organizing anything and everything. He called his framework LATCH, which stands for the five methods: Location, Alphabet, Time, Category, and Hierarchy. Let's look at how each of these methods might work on the web.

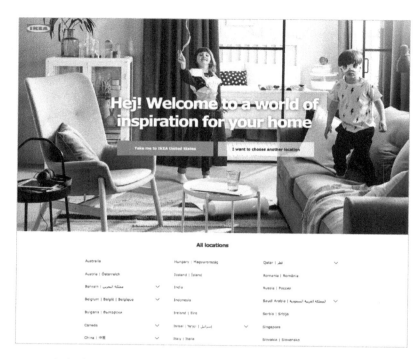

FIG 1.1: The landing page at ikea.com is a list of country-specific sites. At the highest level, IKEA's content is organized by geographic location.

Location

Our first method is organization by location—for instance, atlases, city maps, and bus routes are all organized by location. That paper map you pick up at the entrance to IKEA before you enter its furniture maze? Locational organization yet again—so you can know *exactly* where you are when your relationship falls apart over a KALLAX bookshelf.

But maps aren't the only way we can organize by location. Location is often a primary organizing principle for digital ecosystems—think Craigslist or Yelp. Like many other global brands, IKEA's website first asks visitors to select their country, to ensure they're being shown the most geographically appropriate version of the content (**FIG 1.1**).

FIG 1.2: IKEA's products are organized according to room—mostly. Categories like Childrens, Lighting, and Wireless charging break the locational model (and editorial style guide).

After clicking into the IKEA United States site, the content is, again, organized according to location—but, this time, not geographically. The Products menu is organized by room: bedroom, kitchen, living room (**FIG 1.2**). The navigation is structured according to visitors' mental models of homes.

Be careful—just because information is geographical in nature does not mean location should be its organizing principle. A list of state capitals, for instance, is a list of literal locations, but is probably better organized alphabetically. Meanwhile, a list of butcher cuts would be better presented as a ~~forearm tattoo~~ diagram—that is, a locationally organized illustration—despite having nothing to do with geography.

Alphabet

Almost as soon as we learn the alphabet, we're taught to start structuring information by it. When we're young, we hear our teachers take attendance according to our classmates' last names; we're taught vocabulary words in alphabetized lists; we're told to look up spellings in the dictionary.

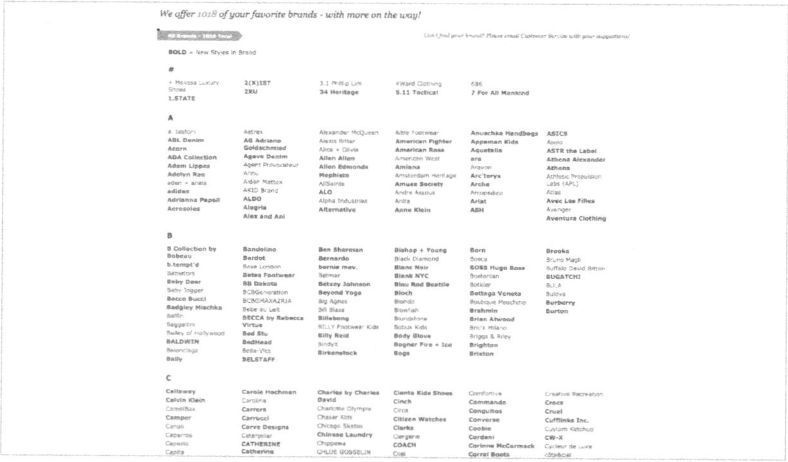

We offer 1018 of your favorite brands - with more on the way!

FIG 1.3: Listing over one thousand brands alphabetically would be a terrible way to browse shoes—but it's perfect for finding a specific brand name.

When it comes to web content, though, alphabetical organization is rarely used at high levels—you just don't see navigation menus A-Z. Instead, it's reserved for information retrieval, because it facilitates finding a needle in a data haystack.

The alphabet, as a preexisting, equalizing structure, provides the quickest path to a single, known item within a very long list. Think of dictionaries, an index in the back of the book, or the contact list in your phone. Or think of Zappos, an ecommerce giant with an equally giant inventory: the only sensible way to view all brands at once is in an alphabetized list (**FIG 1.3**).

Of course, it's not sensible to view all brands at once, anyway—unless you need to find one specific brand among a thousand. Such an overwhelming list is hardly an enticing method of browsing, but it isn't meant to be. Alphabetizing isn't for discovery—it's for research.

Because of this, make sure you're only using alphabetical organization when you're certain your users already know what they're looking for.

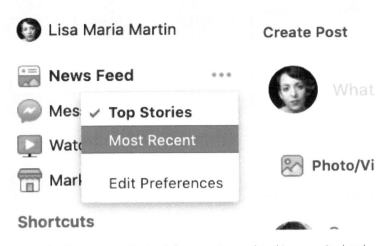

FIG 1.4: Every day, for years now, Facebook forces me to complete this arcane ritual, and still the blood oath has not been sealed.

Time

We organize a *ton* of content by time-based factors: calendars, horoscopes, meeting agendas. Our email inboxes are sorted by recency of message, because anything else would be cruel and unusable. Social media feeds are (almost by definition) time-based—we expect to see tweets, for instance, in reverse-chronological order, with newer messages ceding to older ones as we continue to scroll. (Not that Twitter necessarily cares what we expect to see (http://bkaprt.com/eia/01-02/).)

Not every social media platform handles its feed this way. Facebook keeps defaulting to the Top Stories display, forcing me to toggle a switch daily to keep my feed as chronological as possible (**FIG 1.4**)—without it, a deeply opaque algorithm throws time out the window.

This practice is disruptive because time is an inherent factor in the reading and writing of social posts. Imagine asking for dinner recommendations for a city you'll be visiting for just two days, only to see responses the day after you've returned home.

Online, time is of the essence. What happens in the moment needs to be responded to in the moment.

Even if the content isn't time-sensitive, per se, timing still matters: it adds context that helps users better understand the content. A news item may have longevity beyond its publication date, but knowing that date is part of what helps readers determine relevancy. Even if the topic of the writing is evergreen, a publication date helps readers locate it in a particular cultural or historical moment.

This is why news organizations use time as a primary organizing principle. It's not just that timely equals good, or recent equals SEO. It's that time adds meaning. *When* a piece of content was published changes how it's understood.

Category

Organizing by category means organizing around topics, themes, or other predetermined groupings. Grocery stores are organized categorically: produce is grouped together, dairy is grouped together, cereal is grouped together. (My local store recently added an extra banana display in the cereal aisle. I objected on sight, but then I remembered I'd forgotten to grab bananas in the produce section. You win this time, Stop and Shop.)

The vast majority of website navigation is organized categorically—section labels like About Us or Our Products are categories. You may have noticed that Amazon (like pretty much all retailers) uses categories to organize its product lists (FIG 1.5).

Categorical organization is often more flexible and robust than location or alphabet. It's excellent for breaking down large data sets into smaller, more usable, more *findable* pieces. That makes it perfect for discovery, especially around products, music, and movies.

What better illustration of this idea than Netflix, that wily minx famous for its hyper-specific genre labels (FIG 1.6)? Browsing categories like Oddballs & Outcasts, Quirky TV Shows Featuring a Strong Female Lead, and Unlikely Friends Comedies makes it easy to find new programs well-suited to my

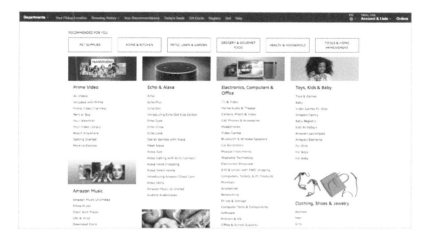

FIG 1.5: Amazon's full product list uses multiple levels of categories to help users find what they're looking for.

FIG 1.6: Ugh, *Bleach*? Definitely not my preferred anime subgenre ("Handsome Figure Skaters Who Kiss Sometimes").

tastes, programs I might not have discovered otherwise. (Yes, those are all from my own feed. Yes, I have a type.) The category system sometimes makes it easier to find specific programs, too. Typing in a search query is slow; it's much faster to navigate to *Kill la Kill* when it's on display in the Anime category, and heaven knows I don't like to wait for my sentient-military-uniform cartoon.

On the other hand, these buck-wild categories can also complicate a more traditional browsing experience. Niche categories make for narrower appeal; the algorithm rarely suggests anything outside of my perceived viewing habits, even if I want something unexpected. New releases get replaced by even newer releases, so if I miss something one week, I may never spot it again. In many ways, this can *hinder* discovery.

Turns out I'm not the only one with this problem: entire websites have been devoted to cataloguing Netflix genres, most of which would only be accessible by the whims of algorithm. URL codes for thousands of categories—organized (alphabetically!) from Action & Adventure Based on a Book from the 1960s, to Zombies—means more direct access for viewers than the Netflix interface provides (http://bkaprt.com/eia/01-03/).

With that much content, categorical organization is an absolute necessity. Just don't fall into the trap of believing categories are the final word—other elements of design, functionality, and strategy have to help make categories *useful*.

Hierarchy

Hierarchy, the last of Wurman's five methods, is about arranging items according to value: from least to most or most to least. The key to understanding this method is that it requires *value* to be assigned to the information.

Sometimes that value is an inherent quality of the information. Yarn shop Eat.Sleep.Knit allows users to search for yarns in its inventory by brand, by color, by fiber, and also by weight—that last one being a hierarchical organization. Knitters and crocheters know that the lightest yarn available is lace-weight, and the heaviest is super bulky; displaying yarn weights

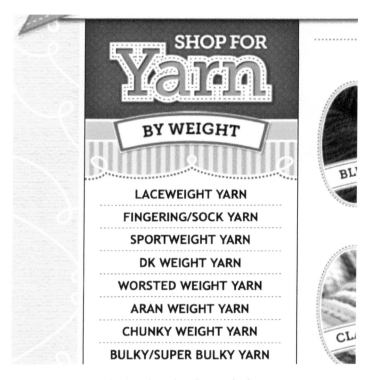

FIG 1.7: To someone who doesn't work with yarn, this list may not appear to have any order at all; but to a knitter, it's a well-known hierarchy, and any other order would be confusing.

in order of lightest to heaviest matches the mental model held by Eat.Sleep.Knit's audience (**FIG. 1.7**).

In other cases, hierarchy is determined by *imposing* values onto data. On a social platform, or on a publication's website, a list of "Most Popular" content is typically a hierarchical selection based on analytics. Popularity, as deemed by the powers that be, rules. See also: Facebook's Top Stories display that I complained about a few pages back. See also: Instagram.

Oh, Instagram, what am I gonna do with you? What should be a time-based system has been warped into an algorithmically driven guessing game: was this posted ten seconds ago

FIG 1.8: A post from "5 hours ago" followed by a post from "12 minutes ago." This is chaotic evil.

 parisianfloors @_ladie_di_ i am happy I could share that and that you enjoyed it

5 HOURS AGO

smittenkitchen ...

1,355 likes

smittenkitchen These cookies are crisp-edged, soft within, finished with a faint crunch of sea salt and absolutely puddled with more

Load more comments

oklahoma_red_bird Everything you cook/ bake is PERFECTION!!!!!!

hcpowl number one best cookie 🤍

suzygerstein @trishacole you literally JUST read my mind 🍴💁🍪📱🌀

leeleela @alex_cherry

12 MINUTES AGO

 travismcelroy ...

Eddie
@HoopsOverhoes

Follow

All we want is to get the pictures back in chronological order...

Complex @Complex
Instagram is reportedly preparing to allow videos up to an hour long. trib.al/WzvHq2d

2:42 PM - 6 Jun 2018

95,986 Retweets 361,368 Likes

280   96K   361K

FIG 1.9: Please. Instagram. We're begging you.

or ten days ago? Am I seeing my friends' pictures or endless ads for bras?

The posts in my feed appear where they do not because of recency (five hours ago, twelve minutes ago), or even relevancy, but because the system allotted weight to them (FIG 1.8). They are organized by a hierarchy only Instagram knows—it's hidden from the user, separate from the user's preferences (FIG 1.9).

One final warning about organization by hierarchy: please don't confuse this with the concepts of *page* hierarchy or *information* hierarchy. The former deals with how web pages are arranged within your system (i.e. sitemaps!), and the latter is consideration for the relative importance of information in a given environment. Hierarchy, as an organizational method, is about the order of the information itself.

IMPERFECT SYSTEMS

LATCH is not a flawless system. Upon deeper inspection, it contains an awful lot of subjectivity and contradiction. Is a grocery store truly organized by category, or does the labeling of aisles suggest a locational approach? Does organizing yarn by color reflect a categorical system, or is color an additional method left out of the acronym? (LATCCH?)

In a 2012 blog post, information professional Katherine Bertolucci identified multiple flaws like these—starting with the idea that LATCH itself is organized *mnemonically*, a method Wurman didn't include (http://bkaprt.com/eia/01-04/). (LAMTCCH?)

There is also a case to be made for differentiating between methods of *grouping* and methods of *ordering*. Location, Alphabet, and Time, Bertolucci pointed out, are all ordering methods, but Category is a grouping method: once categories are made, they still need to be ordered. To recall an earlier example, Netflix uses categorical organization to create groups like Anime or British TV Shows—but how did they decide which categories to show me, and in what order (FIG 1.6)?

We could argue that this is hierarchical, as in our Instagram example; we could argue that anything not transparent to the user, anything derived by way of complex algorithm, reflects a hierarchy of corporate valuation. But it's also fair to say that LATCH has some gaps and logical missteps.

Bertolucci pointed out another gap: organization by way of shape. (SLAMTCCH? Okay, I'll stop.) This is particularly relevant in the world of digital design, because—let's all just admit it—sometimes we *do* make structural decisions based on fit, or layout, or, heck, just a gut feeling that something *looks* like it should be structured that way. Just because a method is aggressively subjective does not make it less of a method!

STARTING POINTS

LATCH is not perfect, nor is it the *only* framework available for thinking about organization and structure. But it's useful because it gives us a springboard for exploring different approaches. It's comforting to know that there is a finite number of ways to organize infinite information—even if we disagree over what that number is.

This is not about committing LATCH to memory, nor about choosing the One True Framework for organizing your website. The LATCH methods may not provide a solution for your specific web content. On the other hand, they might fit perfectly— or at least shed new light on your organizational approaches.

The important thing is to recognize that organizational frameworks exist—that organization is *never* arbitrary.

More to my point: it *can't* be arbitrary, because every decision we make—or fail to make—changes the way the information is perceived. To create organizational structures that are the most effective for our users, we have to start with the meaning of the information—the content itself. And the only way to do that is to get up close and personal with what it is we need to organize.

2 CONTENT ANALYSIS

UNDERSTANDING THE CONTENT OF A SITE is such a basic step, such an *early* step, that it's easy to overlook—and then, miles down the road, phases later in a project, we end up with poor spacing, overflowing headlines, out-of-sync templates, and unintended gaps.

In other words: things don't *fit*, because we made design decisions based on assumptions. We assumed we knew what the content said. We assumed we knew its scope, its patterns, its structures. And now we've caused project problems for our colleagues, and usability problems for our users. *We can't keep doing this.*

Someone on the project needs to be the advocate for the content. Someone needs to know it. Not memorize it, not read-every-single-page-until-your-eyes-cross, but understand what exists and what it means. That person could be you! It doesn't have to be you. But hey, you're already here. Welcome, new content advocate. You're among friends.

You can't organize what you don't understand. Before you can begin to work with the information on a website, in *any* capacity, you have to evaluate it. And by that, I mean: let's conduct some audits (airhorn).

GETTING STARTED WITH AUDITS

Audits impose order on chaos. At the start of a project, a website can seem like a shapeless force, an overwhelming void sucking in all the light, defying knowledge of its inner workings. But audits are your way in.

My enthusiasm for audits—and their related artifacts, like spreadsheets and reports—lies somewhere in the Leslie Knope / Amy Santiago range, and I'm self-aware enough to know that's not like *most* people. But if you can't love audits, I hope you can learn to appreciate their nitty-gritty, multicelled majesty.

Or, at least, their results: from the tiniest atoms of content insight, to the most sweeping experiential conclusions, all the data you collect from an audit will power your project. Audits help you define scopes, target vulnerabilities, and identify strengths. They give you the information you need to make sound design decisions.

But to get that information—before you even begin the auditing itself—you need to make sure you're collecting the right kind of data for the right reasons.

"Who cares about old content?"

Record scratch: I realize some of you might be thinking, "I don't need to do an audit! My client/boss/team has decided we're scrapping the content and starting fresh! Why waste time on content we don't want?"

Do it anyway. For two reasons:

1. Rarely can content be *entirely* scrapped. Even when stake-holders say they're "starting fresh," they often change their tune when the time comes to create new content. Revising can be easier (and more cost-effective) than writing from scratch. And there's equity built into the current content—your users, search engines, and content owners are already familiar with it. Take advantage of that, and build from it, instead of chucking it wholesale!

2. To build a new and improved system, you must first understand the strengths and weakness of what came before. As information architect Jorge Arango wrote on his blog, "You must observe the functioning system for a long time to develop a useful mental model. (Useful in that it helps you make reasonable predictions about what's coming next.) (http://bkaprt.com/eia/02-01/)"

If you are building a brand-new website or product, you may not have web content to analyze immediately—but still, there will be content eventually, and that content should be assessed and accounted for. No matter the current or intended state of content, there is value in analyzing it.

Audit definitions

An *audit* is any critical review of a website. You've probably conducted audits, informally or otherwise, of, say, interface modules, or design patterns. There are as many types of audits, and as many ways of *doing* audits, as there are websites.

I don't want to get too prescriptive about audit terminology, but I do want to clarify a couple dichotomies that could lead us astray.

Audits versus inventories

First, I want to underscore the difference between a *content audit* and a *content inventory*, two terms that are unfortunately and frequently confused.

An audit is a *process*; an inventory is a *product*. An audit is the *action* of reviewing a website; an inventory is the *artifact* that results from the audit.

Please keep these terms separate! Making a distinction between process and product is incredibly useful—it helps clients and colleagues understand the difference between the grind and the output. Plus, it's easier for everyone when we're working from the same shared vocabulary.

Qualitative versus quantitative

Traditionally (inasmuch as the disciplines of the web can claim tradition), we talk about audits as either *qualitative* or *quantitative*. A qualitative audit is focused on the quality of the content: criteria like readability, voice and tone, how well it matches the brand. A quantitative audit, in contrast, is focused on numbers: how many pages, how many images, how many words.

But (drumroll) that's a false dichotomy. *All* audits have a mix of qualitative and quantitative factors—at least, all the audits that have ever been useful to me. What good is a bunch of numbers without a story? What does quality matter without some measurements to contextualize it?

Automated versus manual

Another distinction you might have heard about is *automated* versus *manual* audits. Automated audits (sometimes called *crawls*) are conducted by a robot—software that combs a given domain and returns data about the pages found there. In contrast, manual audits are conducted by, well, you.

At first blush, automated audits seem *swell*—let the robots do the work! Who wants to review thousands of pages? *Who has that kind of time?* Automated tools seem not only faster, but more accurate; audits conducted by *real people* will suffer from the biases and errors of those real people, but robots are made of *science*. How could anyone resist?

But relying solely on automated audits is like thinking your audit is solely quantitative. Data only tells half the story. You need human oversight to fill in context and make sense of the cold, hard numbers.

Auditing for purpose

What I'm trying to tell you is that the best audits are going to use a blend of methodologies. The specific mix is determined by *why* you're conducting the audit.

Audits should be purpose-driven. When you know what you're looking to get out of the audit, and what you're going

to do with the data once you have it, then the *type* of audit doesn't really matter—what matters is that you're gathering the information you need.
Here are the starter questions to ask yourself:

- **What's prompting the audit?** Are you starting a redesign? Preparing for a migration? Updating brand standards?
- **What are you trying to learn?** "Number of pages" is a good start, but you may also want to know about content distribution, site structure, URL patterns, content types, etc.
- **Who needs to use the results of the audit (besides you)?** Is a coworker depending on the data to inform their sitemap, their templates, their migration plans? Will it be used to sell or justify additional work?
- **What kind of resources are available for the audit?** Do you have time to work on it (even if you're just barely eking it out)? Would automated tools or additional workers help you?

You might use an automated audit to generate a content inventory so you can prepare for a CMS migration. Or you might use that same automated audit to guide a manual review of page hierarchies. Or maybe you want a more informal, qualitative look at image and video metadata as part of an accessibility audit. *It all depends on your purpose.*

In my work, I often run multiple interconnected audits over the course of a project: first, a simple audit to scope the website; then an automated audit combined with manual scrutiny to inform strategy recommendations; then, finally, a structural audit to lay the foundation for a new sitemap (which we'll talk about in Chapter 4). Each audit builds on the one that came before it. Let's look at how we can layer audits to—really and truly—analyze a site's content.

SCOPING THE SITE

Conducting an audit early in the project—whether to inform a sales pitch, or as part of your discovery work—is an excellent way to scope the content and structural needs of a website and, by extension, the project itself. While I can't guarantee you'll never overpromise and underdeliver again, I can tell you that a quick, high-level audit is a good way to prepare for the challenges ahead.

Maybe this is so obvious it doesn't merit saying, but I'm going to say it anyway: *not all sites have the same content challenges.* I've worked with clients whose biggest hurdle was producing enough content, while others produced so much they struggled to support it. Still others were writing the perfect amount, but had no editorial guidelines—and it showed.

Content and structural challenges are often specific to that organization's way of doing business. Even a relatively quick spin through a website can teach you a lot about a company's values, priorities, publishing practices, technical limitations, and oversights (not to mention its org chart).

And the more you know about those obstacles up front—before you start designing or coding—the more prepared you'll be. A high-level scoping audit can help you arrange for the right resources, set more appropriate timelines, and communicate the right constraints to stakeholders.

Determining scope

When I audit for scope, I am trying to answer several questions:

1. How much content is on the site?
2. What kind of content is it?
3. How is the site structured?
4. How effective is the content?
5. How is the content managed?

I don't need detailed answers—I just need to make an educated guess about the type and amount of structural work to come. Still, these are big, bad questions that we need to unpack.

How much content is on the site?

Sometimes when people say "scope," they mean "How many pages exist?" That's certainly an important question (and you definitely want a clear answer), but, remember, a number is not the whole story.

Answering this question starts even before the audit: whoever is running the project should know what digital properties are involved. Even if the project scope is "just" the website, it pays to be aware of the other entities in a company's content ecosystem. Social media feeds might be pulled in. Third-party applications might extend the content. There might be a plan to bring an external blog in-house, or move site-hosted photos to a Flickr account. Just because something is or isn't on the site *at this moment* doesn't guarantee its placement in the future.

Discuss with stakeholders exactly which properties and platforms are involved in the redesign, as well as any expected changes to content locations and formats on the horizon. *Then* you can get to quantifying pages.

And as far as that goes, don't fret too much over "big" versus "small" sites. A 100,000-page site will definitely require more time and resources than a 100-page site, but you won't find huge scoping differences between, say, 5,000 and 10,000 pages.

Besides, more challenging scoping factors will likely emerge from the *kind* of content on the site.

What kind of content is it?

Try to get a sense of some of the different content types or styles that currently exist. On an ecommerce site, you can expect product descriptions, support forums, and company news. A university will likely have a mix of marketing content for prospective students and evergreen content for current students. A nonprofit might have a lot of advocacy content and financial documentation.

You're looking for patterns, such as:

- How much content is evergreen versus dynamic?
- Is the content focused on marketing? Is it selling a product or service?
- Are there articles, blog posts, interviews, or other journalistic writing (what I term *storytelling content*)?

- Is the content research-based? Are there white papers and reports? How is it distributed or made available to users?
- Is there a lot of documentation or support content? How is it distributed or made available to users?
- Are there forums, bulletin boards, or other community-based content areas?
- What kind of rich media (images, videos, slideshows, social media integration, etc.) does the site have?

For example, a site with a big news gallery and lots of images may indicate challenges with chronological browsing, image performance, or publishing workflows, while a site with an extensive research database may struggle with PDF accessibility, outdated content, or readability.

You don't need to produce an exhaustive list (or any solutions!)—you're just looking for the broad strokes, a sense of what you might need to dig into later.

How is the site structured?

You're not conducting an in-depth structural audit yet, but pay attention to structural clues throughout the site:

- Is it easy to navigate, or do you get lost quickly?
- Do the URLs match the expected paths?
- Are there breadcrumbs and other wayfinding features?
- Are any areas duplicated or missing from the menus?
- Can you easily understand the relationships between pages?
- Are pages with similar content constructed the same way?
- Does content flow logically on each page?
- Do things generally work the way you expect them to?

If you're seeing a lot of inconsistency in the structures and navigation mechanisms, that's a sign that your project will require more heavy lifting around the information architecture.

How effective is the content?

As you begin to develop a sense of what the content is, keep an eye on its quality. You don't need to read every page on the site—you want a representative sample of high-profile landing pages, pages with heavy stakeholder investment, and low-level pages that don't often see the light of day.

Is the content easy to read? Is it clear? Is it helpful? It is full of typos? Does it sound like the brand it purports to be? Don't get too in the weeds here—but if you're seeing a lot of challenges around the quality of the content, you may want to talk to your team or client about adding a dedicated content strategy effort to the scope. (More on that in a moment.)

Poor-quality content can indicate a range of behind-the-scenes challenges around publishing processes, quality control, resource allocation, and leadership. It's often the mark of a company that doesn't want to put their money where their mouth is—which becomes obvious as soon as you start digging into how the content is managed.

How is the content managed?

Sometimes the biggest challenge in content is the workflow behind it: how content is written and edited, how it's published in the CMS, and how it's governed over time.

This is a tricky question because it's not something you can discern from the audit (except via correlated quality issues). But you can identify content management challenges in stakeholder interviews. Talk to the people at the top (usually the ones driving the initiative) as well as the people in the trenches (i.e. the content authors). Ask them what their biggest content pain points are, and I'm betting you'll hear answers like:

- There aren't dedicated content authors, and no budget or plans to hire writers.
- Content authors don't have enough time to write.
- Authors don't have permissions in the CMS, or authors don't know how to use the CMS.

- There's no documentation of editorial guidelines or CMS processes, or no resources or budget to train authors.
- There isn't enough (or any) editorial oversight, so there's no consistency in content quality, editorial style, or voice.
- There's too much editorial oversight, so publishing is a slow, bottlenecked process.

No matter how beautiful the new site is, no matter how thoughtfully you create a sitemap, no matter how accessible and functional it all turns out to be—if an organization does not address the way it approaches its content, the new website will fall into the same disrepair as the old one.

That doesn't mean there's no hope! Plenty of website projects get off the ground in less than ideal conditions. (All of them, in fact.) Just remember that you may have to temper your content expectations when you get into the design phase—which is why you're scoping with an audit up front.

Planning your resources

Once you've completed your (brief, high-level, likely informal) scoping audit, you should have a sense of the biggest content and structural challenges in front of you—so you can start to plan for additional project tasks, deliverables, or staffing. For instance:

- If your scoping audit demonstrated a lot of challenges around the quality or nature of the content, you may want to bring in a content strategist to consult.
- If you saw lots of editorial or publishing challenges in the audit, you may need to hire more copywriters, or plan for more training.
- Lots of navigation and wayfinding obstacles suggest you'll need to prepare for intense systems thinking.

And while you might want to hire specialists to help you tackle these problems and more, you might also, well, not.

The whole point of this book, actually, is that *you* can do many of these tasks. In an ideal world, dedicated information architects and content strategists would be included on every digital product from here to eternity. But I am nothing if not practical, and I know hiring another employee or consultant isn't always in the cards.

Sometimes, when teams are faced with content challenges and inadequate support, they'll dismiss or minimize the obstacles ahead by saying things like:

- **"The site's not that big."** There's no magic number of pages where, suddenly, "content work" is warranted—the tasks are the same at any size. What changes is the scale, depth, and complexity of the problems (and solutions). A huge site may require multiple content managers handling specialized tasks, but a tiny site still needs someone advocating for the content and responsible structural decisions.
- **"The content's not that complicated."** I'll give you this: not every website is about nuclear nonproliferation. Sometimes the website covers a really familiar topic, or is selling a well-known product, or we ourselves fall into the target audience. But perceived simplicity of subject has nothing to do with, well, anything—the most straightforward content in the world can still fall victim to any number of organizational misdemeanors.
- **"The client / the other team is handling it."** While it's nice to delegate tasks to someone else, there's no substitute for your own understanding. If you wash your hands of the content, you'll be working from an incomplete picture of the problem space. And that's the *best*-case scenario—more often, the client or other team won't have a complete picture themselves. Content owners rarely have an objective sense of their structural challenges, the impact on design and development work, or the resources they'll need to allocate.

I get it: content is hard, and resources are scarce, and timelines are tight, and problems usually just go away if you ignore them. Right?

But it benefits both you and the project to plan for the content and structural needs of the site—so you can collaborate with content creators and stakeholders, recommend resources, and build a better user experience all around.

If your team has the budget to hire a dedicated content strategist or information architect, that's great. But if not, I want to make sure that *you* can make informed, responsible, effective structural decisions. Let's keep going.

WORKING WITH AUTOMATED DATA

Once you've scoped your site at a high level, you can move on to a more detailed audit—one that will provide you with a better view of the current content landscape.

For me, that usually means conducting an automated crawl, paired with a more detailed manual review. The automated data acts as quantitative support for my observations, while the observations give me context for interpreting the data.

The automated crawl tool is also how I build an exhaustive *content inventory*. We defined that earlier as the output of the audit; it's literally a spreadsheet with an entry for every page in your website. That spreadsheet can play a crucial role in building a sitemap, identifying templates, supporting a migration, or any other task that requires a list of pages.

There are many different services or apps you can use to run an automated audit (see the Resources section). Depending on your customization options, the tool you use might collect data like the number of links per page, the number of words per page, the character length of the headings, even data about readability and Google Analytics.

Whatever tool you choose, know that the results are going to require some finessing. They're often, well, *nonsense* right out of the gate—you'll need to format the spreadsheet so you can read it, and exclude unnecessary data from your analysis.

Making the data usable

Working with automated crawl data is ultimately about translation: how do you make meaning out of a million cells filled with a million numbers (**FIG 2.1**)?

	A	B	C	D	E	F	G	H	I	J	K	L	M	N	O	P	Q
1	URL	DNS Safe U	F Path	Domain	Root Doma	TLD	Scheme	HTTP Sta	HTTP Sta	Original	Original	Original	Content	Content	Charset	Encoding	Hash
2	http://www	http://www	/	www.getty	gettysburg	edu	http	200	OK	http://w	200	OK	text/htn	24486	UTF-8	utf-8	0cf5dd6c1
3	http://www	http://www	/	www.getty	gettysburg	edu	http	200	OK	http://w	200	OK	text/htn	27467	UTF-8	utf-8	e51b1eac1
4	http://www	http://www	/about/	www.getty	gettysburg	edu	http	200	OK	http://w	200	OK	text/htn	27180	UTF-8	utf-8	baa76a715
5	http://www	http://www	/error_page	www.getty	gettysburg	edu	http	200	OK	http://w	302	Redirect	text/htn	17173	UTF-8	utf-8	7f12d0adc
6	http://www	http://www	/about/	www.getty	gettysburg	edu	http	200	OK	http://w	200	OK	text/htn	29913	UTF-8	utf-8	d7f187e4c
7	http://www	http://www	/about/coll	www.getty	gettysburg	edu	http	200	OK	http://w	200	OK	text/htn	24639	UTF-8	utf-8	3bd03b2c5
8	http://www	http://www	/about/coll	www.getty	gettysburg	edu	http	200	OK	http://w	200	OK	text/htn	29913	UTF-8	utf-8	ac60c8572
9	http://www	http://www	/about/coll	www.getty	gettysburg	edu	http	200	OK	http://w	200	OK	text/htn	26305	UTF-8	utf-8	925dbbe32
10	http://www	http://www	/about/coll	www.getty	gettysburg	edu	http	200	OK	http://w	200	OK	text/htn	26432	UTF-8	utf-8	e42b02d9f
11	http://www	http://www	/about/coll	www.getty	gettysburg	edu	http	200	OK	http://w	200	OK	text/htn	25102	UTF-8	utf-8	76f2121e1
12	http://www	http://www	/about/coll	www.getty	gettysburg	edu	http	200	OK	http://w	200	OK	text/htn	25047	UTF-8	utf-8	6c2949404
13	http://www	http://www	/about/coll	www.getty	gettysburg	edu	http	200	OK	http://w	200	OK	text/htn	25400	UTF-8	utf-8	17072e2c0
14	http://www	http://www	/about/coll	www.getty	gettysburg	edu	http	200	OK	http://w	200	OK	text/htn	25159	UTF-8	utf-8	77a923fcct
15	http://www	http://www	/about/coll	www.getty	gettysburg	edu	http	200	OK	http://w	200	OK	text/htn	25245	UTF-8	utf-8	b5d4b117a
16	http://www	http://www	/about/coll	www.getty	gettysburg	edu	http	200	OK	http://w	200	OK	text/htn	25749	UTF-8	utf-8	6d7a9013b
17	http://www	http://www	/about/coll	www.getty	gettysburg	edu	http	200	OK	http://w	200	OK	text/htn	25184	UTF-8	utf-8	e198cf83e
18	http://www	http://www	/about/coll	www.getty	gettysburg	edu	http	200	OK	http://w	200	OK	text/htn	25830	UTF-8	utf-8	45c92c9ea
19	http://www	http://www	/about/coll	www.getty	gettysburg	edu	http	200	OK	http://w	200	OK	text/htn	25351	UTF-8	utf-8	3d5cbedeb
20	http://www	http://www	/about/coll	www.getty	gettysburg	edu	http	200	OK	http://w	200	OK	text/htn	25267	UTF-8	utf-8	c414a3b67
21	http://www	http://www	/about/coll	www.getty	gettysburg	edu	http	200	OK	http://w	200	OK	text/htn	25600	UTF-8	utf-8	6e8be310d
22	http://www	http://www	/about/coll	www.getty	gettysburg	edu	http	200	OK	http://w	200	OK	text/htn	25338	UTF-8	utf-8	066839e28
23	http://www	http://www	/about/coll	www.getty	gettysburg	edu	http	200	OK	http://w	200	OK	text/htn	25973	UTF-8	utf-8	8dc92874b
24	http://www	http://www	/about/coll	www.getty	gettysburg	edu	http	200	OK	http://w	200	OK	text/htn	25336	UTF-8	utf-8	64ebef55e4
25	http://www	http://www	/about/coll	www.getty	gettysburg	edu	http	200	OK	http://w	200	OK	text/htn	33333	UTF-8	utf-8	fc1c5c49f2
26	http://www	http://www	/about/coll	www.getty	gettysburg	edu	http	200	OK	http://w	200	OK	text/htn	28482	UTF-8	utf-8	3f9417d45
27	http://www	http://www	/about/coll	www.getty	gettysburg	edu	http	200	OK	http://w	200	OK	text/htn	26180	UTF-8	utf-8	33cbf479e
28	http://www	http://www	/about/coll	www.getty	gettysburg	edu	http	200	OK	http://w	200	OK	text/htn	24490	UTF-8	utf-8	2c8d42304
29	http://www	http://www	/about/coll	www.getty	gettysburg	edu	http	200	OK	http://w	200	OK	text/htn	24744	UTF-8	utf-8	c1f55eccca
30	http://www	http://www	/about/coll	www.getty	gettysburg	edu	http	200	OK	http://w	200	OK	text/htn	27482	UTF-8	utf-8	e4afa3edc9
31	http://www	http://www	/about/coll	www.getty	gettysburg	edu	http	200	OK	http://w	200	OK	text/htn	24906	UTF-8	utf-8	6f05f1650C
32	http://www	http://www	/error_page	www.getty	gettysburg	edu	http	200	OK	http://w	302	Redirect	text/htn	17173	UTF-8	utf-8	7f12d0adc
33	http://www	http://www	/about/	www.getty	gettysburg	edu	http	200	OK	http://w	200	OK	text/htn	24959	UTF-8	utf-8	07940b06
34	http://www	http://www	/error_page	www.getty	gettysburg	edu	http	200	OK	http://w	302	Redirect	text/htn	17173	UTF-8	utf-8	7f12d0adc
35	http://www	http://www	/about/con	www.getty	gettysburg	edu	http	200	OK	http://w	200	OK	text/htn	24959	UTF-8	utf-8	07940b06
36	http://www	http://www	/about/	www.getty	gettysburg	edu	http	200	OK	http://w	200	OK	text/htn	27467	UTF-8	utf-8	e51b1eac1
37	http://www	http://www	/about/	www.getty	gettysburg	edu	http	200	OK	http://w	200	OK	text/htn	31798	UTF-8	utf-8	323a13d9a
38	http://www	http://www	/about/offi	www.getty	gettysburg	edu	http	200	OK	http://w	200	OK	text/htn	15724	UTF-8	utf-8	5110747e9
39	http://www	http://www	/about/offi	www.getty	gettysburg	edu	http	200	OK	http://w	200	OK	text/htn	28932	UTF-8	utf-8	84e72f07b
40	http://www	http://www	/about/offi	www.getty	gettysburg	edu	http	200	OK	http://w	200	OK	text/htn	28932	UTF-8	utf-8	84e72f07b

FIG 2.1: Please unsubscribe me from this mailing list.

You have to turn that data from noise into signal—something that will provide insights for your strategy and design decisions down the road. Here are some steps I take to make my initial data workable:

- **Style the sheet.** It's hard to read data that's visually disorganized, so spruce it up: apply a different color and text size to the header row, freeze the first row and column, and change the size of the cells to best display the data within them (**FIG 2.2**).
- **Delete or hide unnecessary columns.** There are probably going to be columns with empty data (crawls work in mysterious ways), or columns of data that you just don't need for this audit. Get rid of 'em. If you're hesitant about losing data, hide the columns instead of deleting; over time, you'll develop a sense of what can go and what should stay.

	A	B	C	D	E	F
1	Address	Status Code	Stat	Section	Title 1	Title 1 Length
2	https://www.gettysburg.edu/about/college_history/	200 OK	About		Gettysburg College - College History	36
3	https://www.gettysburg.edu/about/college_history/alma-mater.dot	200 OK	About		Gettysburg College - Alma Mater	31
4	https://www.gettysburg.edu/about/college_history/mission_statemen	200 OK	About		Gettysburg College - Mission Statement	38
5	https://www.gettysburg.edu/about/college_history/president/	200 OK	About		Gettysburg College - Presidents of Gettysbu	53
6	https://www.gettysburg.edu/about/college_history/president/baugher	200 OK	About		Gettysburg College - Henry Lewis Baugher	40
7	https://www.gettysburg.edu/about/college_history/president/carl_har	200 OK	About		Gettysburg College - Carl Arnold Hanson	39
8	https://www.gettysburg.edu/about/college_history/president/glassick	200 OK	About		Gettysburg College - Charles Etzweiler Glass	47
9	https://www.gettysburg.edu/about/college_history/president/granville	200 OK	About		Gettysburg College - William Anthony Gran	46
10	https://www.gettysburg.edu/about/college_history/president/haaland	200 OK	About		Gettysburg College - Gordon A. Haaland	38
11	https://www.gettysburg.edu/about/college_history/president/hefelbo	200 OK	About		Gettysburg College - Samuel Gring Hefelbov	44
12	https://www.gettysburg.edu/about/college_history/president/henry_h	200 OK	About		Gettysburg College - Henry William Andrew	48
13	https://www.gettysburg.edu/about/college_history/president/krauth.d	200 OK	About		Gettysburg College - Charles Philip Krauth	42
14	https://www.gettysburg.edu/about/college_history/president/langsam	200 OK	About		Gettysburg College - Walter Consuelo Langs	44
15	https://www.gettysburg.edu/about/college_history/president/mcknigh	200 OK	About		Gettysburg College - Harvey Washington Mc	47
16	https://www.gettysburg.edu/about/college_history/president/paul.dot	200 OK	About		Gettysburg College - Willard Stewart Paul	41
17	https://www.gettysburg.edu/about/college_history/president/valentin	200 OK	About		Gettysburg College - Milton Valentine	37
18	https://www.gettysburg.edu/about/college_history/president/will.dot	200 OK	About		Gettysburg College - Katherine Haley Will	41
19	https://www.gettysburg.edu/about/college_history/traditions/	200 OK	About		Gettysburg College - Traditions	31
20	https://www.gettysburg.edu/about/college_history/traditions/all.dot	200 OK	About		Gettysburg College - All Traditions	35
21	https://www.gettysburg.edu/about/college_history/traditions/first-yea	200 OK	About		Gettysburg College - First-Year Walk	36
22	https://www.gettysburg.edu/about/college_history/traditions/founder	200 OK	About		Gettysburg College - Founders Day	33
23	https://www.gettysburg.edu/about/college_history/traditions/founder	200 OK	About		Gettysburg College - Founders Day	33
24	https://www.gettysburg.edu/about/college_history/traditions/thanksg	200 OK	About		Gettysburg College - Thanksgiving Dinner	40
25	https://www.gettysburg.edu/about/college_history/traditions/twilight	200 OK	About		Gettysburg College - Twilight Hour Schedule	43
26	https://www.gettysburg.edu/about/college_history/traditions/twilight	200 OK	About		Gettysburg College - Twilight Hour	34
27	https://www.gettysburg.edu/about/offices/college_life/	200 OK	About		Gettysburg College - Welcome to College Lit	81
28	https://www.gettysburg.edu/about/offices/college_life/calendar/	200 OK	About		Gettysburg College - Calendar	29
29	https://www.gettysburg.edu/about/offices/college_life/care/	200 OK	About		Gettysburg College - Concerned About a Stu	54
30	https://www.gettysburg.edu/about/offices/college_life/care/care-grou	200 OK	About		Gettysburg College - CARE Group Members	39

FIG 2.2: Okay, it's still a spreadsheet with the density of a neutron star, but at least now I know what I'm looking at.

- **Remove bad and duplicate entries.** Even when you set your automated crawl parameters carefully, robots sometimes bring back things you don't want, like a cat depositing a half-eaten mouse at your doorstep. Weed out entries for redirects, 404s, JavaScript and other code, files, and duplicate pages (such as URLs that differ only in their security or a trailing slash). You don't need a list of all potential returns (unless that's your goal!); you want an inventory of real pages to evaluate.
- **Add section data.** Counting pages doesn't get you very far, but showing how those pages are distributed across major site sections opens up a world of analytical possibilities. Most crawl tools can't scrape that data, because "site sections" are, well, made up—do we measure them by the navigation labels, by the menu locations, by the URL folder paths? I choose the latter, personally, so a URL like website.

com/about/history would tell me that the page is in the About section. I add a column to my spreadsheet (sometimes two or three, depending on site depth) and fill in this data manually.

There are many other tweaks I make to the data in service of usability, and you'll find your own tweaks, too—whatever it takes to make the data usable for *you*.

Parsing the data

Once you get the spreadsheet into a workable format, you can start to assess the data. Again, this will depend on the returns of your specific crawl tool, but these are the criteria I usually focus on:

- **Number of pages.** This is where manually adding that section data starts to pay off—you learn not only the size of the site, but the size of each *section*, which is to say, how content is distributed across the site (**FIG 2.3**). This can highlight where content *production* might be outpacing content *value*. For example, a company may say it values educating users— but low numbers in its Support section tell a different story. Relative page counts (plus some workflow insights) show a company's true priorities.
- **Number of images and videos.** Again, relative distribution across sections may point out where content production is out of sync with the stated intention. If your tool also scrapes metadata for images, you can analyze alt text—a crucial point for accessibility discussions.
- **Word count.** Don't be fooled—high word counts aren't automatically bad! It all depends on the type of content, the brand, and the audience. A nonprofit that posts research papers will rack up higher word counts than an app that prides itself on quick, seamless interactions—and to each their own. Again, look at the numbers in context: are there sections where the average word count is much higher or lower than elsewhere? Are the outliers justified, or are they unintentional?

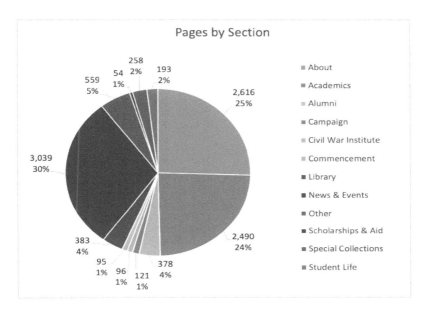

FIG 2.3: My audit for Gettysburg College turned up over ten thousand pages, but it was far more interesting to me to learn that those pages were distributed almost equally across just three sections.

- **Comparative readability.** I don't love readability tests, because they're often used as shortcuts for learning how to recognize good writing. They are also no-good robots— eldritch algorithms cobbled from the linguistic biases of their makers. No readability test can truly assess what it's like for a real human to read real writing in a real context. That said: I *do* look at the readability scores in my automated crawls. My tools use five or six different metrics, so what I examine is not the individual outputs but the *trend* in readability scores across each section (**FIG 2.4**). These trends suggest starting points for additional manual scrutiny.
- **Number of links.** I sound like a broken record at this point, but: look at these numbers relative to their sections, and follow up on statistical outliers. Some crawl tools will cover inlinks (number of links coming into the page), outlinks

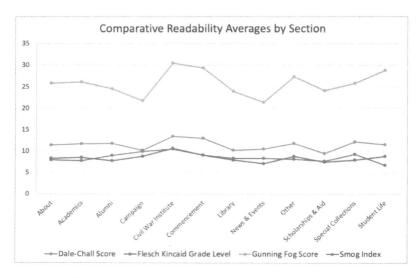

FIG 2.4: The differences in these scores are less important than their consistency. For instance, pages in the News & Events section ranked better in all four tests (lower numbers indicate better comprehensibility); the writing style in that section might serve as a good model when it comes time to revise content.

(number of links on the page to other pages in the domain), and external outlinks (number of links on the page to other domains). That's a lot to consider. But these numbers can provide insight into the connections across the site, or places where users are being accidentally diverted.

How you actually crunch these numbers is up to you, depending on your tools and your knowledge of the dark arts of spreadsheets. I rely on a lot of tabs, elaborate pivot tables, and overwrought charts based on those pivot tables (http:// bkaprt.com/eia/02-02/). No, *you're* the nerd. Shut up.

The data from the automated audit isn't operating on its own, of course; I've also got the observations from my scoping audit, which adds context and suggests places to dig in further. It's this combination that reveals insights I can rely on for the rest of the project. I usually incorporate my findings into a formal report, which informs the design strategy and recommended content approach.

AFTER THE AUDITS

Between your scoping audit and your analysis of automated audit data, you probably now know the information on your website better than anyone.

You've read, you've counted, you've recorded, you've assessed. You've analyzed both the big picture and the gritty details of the system. You've emerged with the wisdom of the ancients, and you are well-positioned to advocate for the informational experience on your site.

I mean, *damn*, Mary—that's a nice bake.

With all of this analytical nose-to-the-grindstone work, let's not lose sight of why we're doing it in the first place. It's all so that future design and development decisions will be grounded in truth, rather than assumptions. They will be decisions that respect the contexts of your content *and* the contexts of your users.

Now that we now the truth of the information, we're more likely to build structures that will effectively communicate it. It's time to start thinking about what those structures might be.

3 CATEGORIES AND LABELS

CHAIN MOTELS, STRIP MALLS, and office parks are deeply mundane buildings, most of us would agree—but not architecture writer Kate Wagner, best known from her blog McMansion Hell. Such buildings might not be remarkable, but they make up our daily landscapes, and therefore deserve our attention.

In a 2018 article, Wagner compared our dismissal of these everyday buildings to "tree blindness," the phenomenon in which we don't notice the trees on our own streets—and, she argued, neither oversight is a good thing: "[B]eing blind to buildings robs us of a deeper level of understanding and interaction" (http://bkaprt.com/eia/03-01/).

I'd argue that we suffer from a similar kind of *structural* blindness on the web. Because the site structure is so intrinsic, so omnipresent, it is easy to ignore. Sitemaps and sections and labels and categories are such givens that we forget they are worthy of deeper attention—of deeper *intention*.

Categorizing content is an important first step in structuring the site—it's the basis for your *sitemap*, the document that codifies that structure. We'll talk about putting the sitemap together in the next chapter; right now, we need to consider the conceptual organization of content, and how we can be more intentional about it.

Thinking back to Chapter 1, we know categorization is one of the LATCH methods for organizing information. And it's an abundant method—just about every website incorporates some kind of categorical distribution of information.

But: *How* do we categorize?

CRITERIA MATCHING

Categorizing web content seems to be incredibly straightforward, at first: just group like items together!

It sounds simple because we—quite naturally—group like items together all the time in our daily lives. Put socks in the drawer with other socks. Put vegetables in the crisper with other vegetables. Put books about web design on the shelf with other books about web design.

But that straightforwardness falls away when we have to define what we mean by "like." Determining "like" is a process of drawing boundaries, of deciding what to include and what to exclude. It's a process fraught with subjectivity, bias, politics, errors, and cultural and historical memory. It's anything *but* simple.

Categorizing content is a process of *criteria matching*, which means we have to answer two questions:

1. What are the criteria for the category?
2. Does the content match the criteria?

The first question starts with the macro view: we need to know the big picture, to understand how all the pieces fit together. (That's why it's so critical to audit the content first.) Once we've defined a category—not just identified it, but established its parameters—we can assess content against that definition, answering the second question.

In real life, we don't perfectly define all categories up front, then assess content against that rigid structure one piece at a time. The process of categorization is much more fluid—we move back and forth between defining the criteria and vetting the criteria, seeing how the details fit in the system and how the system must change to accommodate details. We move constantly between macro and micro views of the content, allowing each to inform the other.

If I'm shopping for peanut butter at my local grocery store, I know I'll find it in the furthest aisle to the left of the door, between the jelly and bread. I don't know how the store refers to it internally, but the criteria for this aisle seems to be "things used to make a peanut butter and jelly sandwich."

But if I go shopping for peanut butter at an unfamiliar grocery store, it usually takes me a few guesses to find it. I might check the condiments aisle, in case the store's criteria is "things you spread on other things." Or I might look near the cereal, in case their criteria is "things you might eat for breakfast."

Each store treats peanut butter a little differently, though within the bounds of logic: they establish categories for their aisles, then determine where to stock the peanut butter based on how it fits the criteria for that aisle. As a user of the grocery store, I need to be able to perceive its decision-making process in order to locate the product I want. (And hence, we need clear aisle signage!)

So it is with websites. Users coming to your site—especially new users—don't necessarily know the big picture of your system *or* the granular details of the content within it. They may see your site as an overwhelming space with too many choices, or a narrow alley with few visible pathways. *They don't know where you've put the peanut butter.*

CATEGORICAL CONSIDERATIONS

We shouldn't simply make up criteria on a whim—we always have reasons for what we do! We need to be able to justify and explain our criteria.

Whenever I need to determine criteria for organizing digital content, I look to four key factors to shape my categorization:

1. The needs of the users
2. The goals of the business
3. The current state of the content
4. The strategic future of the content

Together, these factors help us be deliberate and transparent about categorization, which in turn helps users find the content they need. Let's take a closer look at each.

User needs

Our categories should be informed, like many other decisions made in design, by the needs of our users. Who is on the site? What are they trying to accomplish? What are their primary actions? What do they care about?

By the time you're building categories for web content, you've (presumably) already done the research and discovery work that answers these questions about your users. You already know who's visiting the site; what they want and need should inform the way you organize your content, as well as the language you use to label it.

I recently worked on a website redesign for a nonprofit organization called the Posse Foundation. Their mission is to send kids to college: they identify students with strong leadership potential but who might be overlooked by the traditional college selection process, and then provide them with the financial, academic, social, and professional support they need to succeed in college and beyond.

As you might imagine, an organization like that has a lot of different users: high school students investigating the program, teachers nominating students to participate, university partners providing scholarships, prospective partners who want to get involved. There are donors, volunteers, mentors, recruiters, alumni, board members, steering committees, and staff. Each audience has different tasks, different needs, and different expectations of the content.

A natural reaction to having so many audiences is to categorize content *by* audience. It certainly seems sensible—alumni can click on one label, universities can click on another. That's how the original Posse Foundation website operated (**FIG 3.1**). There are several problems with that approach, however, as many studies have shown (http://bkaprt.com/eia/03-02/, http://bkaprt.com/eia/03-03/):

- Users are visiting to accomplish a specific task—not select an identity. Having to first self-select a label adds an extra step to their path.
- Users aren't confident in how they categorize themselves. They may belong to multiple categories, or none of the visible categories; or they may belong to one but suspect that the content they want is in another.
- Because many audiences—and their tasks—tend to overlap, the content being served in audience-specific categories tends to overlap as well. This leads to duplication, confusing search results, and the potential for errors.

Audience-based navigation is rarely the right solution. Structurally, it's better to examine what users need, rather than who they are; to focus on their actions, rather than their personas. As strategist Gerry McGovern put it:

> *Organizing around the customer means organizing around the task that they want to complete. It's not about products. It's not even about services. If I'm an old person in the wintertime, I want to keep warm. My task is to get warm, not to get services.* (http://bkaprt.com/eia/03-04/)

In the case of the Posse Foundation, this meant examining the verbs. Words like *nominate, recruit, support, mentor, hire, join, donate, inspire*: these could be traced to tasks that users wanted to accomplish on the site. They weren't necessarily a one-to-one match for categorizing content, but they were words that helped transcend audience groups and identify commonalities in user needs.

FIG 3.1: One difficulty with audience-based navigation, as in this example from the Posse Foundation's original website, is that we don't know whether these content areas will feature content *for* those audiences or *about* those audiences.

Business goals

Of course, user needs aren't the *only* consideration on a website—otherwise, something something downfall of capitalism. We have to balance the user needs with the goals of the business. What does the business want to accomplish? What story is it trying to tell? Why are we even doing this work, whether it's a redesign or a page tweak or a product launch? And why now?

The hope, of course, is that the goals of the business align with the needs of the user—that's the desired outcome of any strategy work worth its salt. Provided these items are in alignment, we can push our categorization further in the right direction.

The Posse Foundation had a number of business goals tied to its website. There was, of course, the nonprofit's mission itself, as well as the specific ways the website carried out that mission: allowing teachers to nominate students, allowing donors to contribute money, allowing universities to join the program.

But the primary goal in redesigning the site was to better share the mission and demonstrate their impact—to tell their story. The old site might have expressed it in words, but it wasn't felt in the design—and certainly not in the site structure.

Those main content categories—Our Scholars, Our Alumni, Our University Partners (**FIG 3.1**)—don't tell a story. The only thing they tell a new visitor is that this organization has scholars, alumni, and university partners.

What a missed opportunity! The main sections of a site are just as much a part of the experience as the colors, layout, and content. To group pages without considering the narrative—well, you might as well use your org chart as your navigation.

And to be clear: you shouldn't do that! Org chart navigation is a cliché in the industry because it's such a poor, yet omnipresent, solution. When we talk about incorporating business goals into category-making, that doesn't mean that categories should reflect the business' structure. Users don't care how your business teams function. They just want to complete their tasks. We want to fight against Conway's Law—*organizations that design systems will reproduce their communication structures as those systems*—not give in to it.

Current state

The third factor to consider in categorization is the current state of the content. And since you've conducted such solid audits, you already have the insights you need!

I sometimes hear resistance to using the current content as a factor in *anything*—after all, if a site is being redesigned, why should we pay attention to what we're getting rid of? But, as we discussed in Chapter 2, current content is:

- a good yardstick for predicting future content,
- full of brand equity (companies rarely want to destroy what they've already put years of effort into), and
- all you've got, anyway.

The lessons from the audit should now inform your categories. You learned how the content is currently distributed and categorized, and the strengths and weaknesses of that categorization. You learned what's missing, and what there's too much of. You learned the depth of the site—whether it's wide and shallow, or narrow and deep, or (for those overachiever websites) wide *and* deep.

To get those lessons out plainly, I like to recreate the current sitemap with a simple visualizing tool like Boardthing or Trello or, heck, index cards or sticky notes. Each page or section is represented by a card, color-coded by the top-level content categories (FIG 3.2). The colors themselves don't matter, but you'll want to be able to track the originating categories when you start moving cards into new ones.

FIG 3.2: My initial recreation of the Posse Foundation sitemap on boardthing.com. The hierarchy and connection of the pages wasn't important here, but grouping cards by category (and color) was.

Representing content this way for the Posse Foundation allowed me to see that the site was already well-balanced—it was neither too deep nor too broad, nested only four levels down, and really wasn't very large.

But my research and audit work had shown me that this content, while equally distributed across categories, was not equally *important*. Users were interested in the actions they could take (understanding the nomination process, for example), while stakeholders were interested in program outcomes. Content supporting these interests was limited to just a few pages, hidden a few levels deep.

Why, then, was the most critical information for the site funneled into such a narrow distribution? In fact, everything that both users and stakeholders wanted could be tied back to the same thing: the scholarship lifecycle—the process of nominating, accepting, and supporting students throughout their academic and professional careers (**FIG 3.3**). It was, in fact, a perfect alignment of user needs and business goals—but the site wasn't structured to convey it.

NOMINATION PROCESS

Mission, History, Goals
Why Posse is Needed
Program Components
· Recruitment
· Nomination Process
· Pre-Collegiate Training
· Campus Program
· Career Program
· Posse Access
Specialized Initiatives
Locations
Staff + Board
The Posse Institute
Annual Report

Know an amazing student? We want to know that student, too. If you are a high school or a community-based organization that works with high school juniors/seniors in Atlanta, the Bay Area, Boston, Chicago, Houston, Los Angeles, Miami, New Orleans, New York or Washington, D.C., and you are officially registered with your local Posse office, then you can nominate your students as early as their second semester junior year, in high school. Note that for each Posse location/city, the nomination process may begin in the spring. Please make sure you contact your local Posse office for details at the beginning of every year.

Every year, Posse works closely with its network of high schools and community-based organizations to recruit Posse Scholars. Each Posse Scholar wins a four-year, full-tuition scholarship to attend one of Posse's partner colleges or universities.

REQUIREMENTS

To be eligible, a high school senior MUST:

WHERE IS POSSE?

Posse has chapters in Atlanta, Boston, Chicago, Houston, Los Angeles, Miami, New Orleans, New York and Washington, D.C. Posse opened its 10th chapter in the Bay Area in 2015.

FIG 3.3: The Posse Foundation's program components (bulleted in the left-hand sidebar) were the focal point of all interactions with the organization, yet were compressed on their original website into a single category.

My audit had shown me that content about the scholarship lifecycle existed, even if it was a little bare bones. There was plenty of potential to elevate it in categories that better expressed the user needs *and* business goals.

Future state

The final factor to consider in building content categories is the *intended future* of the content. There are two components to this future state:

- The strategy that's driving the design
- The resources for content creation and maintenance

As we've discussed, your site's categories are part of the experience, which means that your strategy needs to inform your structure. Every organization, agency, and discipline seems to call its strategic guidelines something different—a core statement, a brand playbook, a message architecture, identity pillars,

FIG 3.4: The color-coding I had previously set up made it easy to see how much content shuffling was involved to reach a new potential sitemap. Green cards indicated new content that would need to be developed.

design principles, etc. Whatever you call yours, you've got *something* that's guiding your thinking.

That *something* may suggest that new content needs to be created, that the current content needs to be rewritten, that the content needs to be reshuffled and relabeled, or some combination of all three. For the Posse Foundation, delivering on the tell-the-story strategy meant focusing on their scholarship process: top-level categories that could speak to how students were supported before, during, and after their participation in the program. I wanted the mission of the organization to be articulated in the structure of the site itself (**FIG 3.4**).

Of course, my thinking had to be tempered by the available content resources. The shift in category focus meant that some content would need to be rewritten, metadata would need to be updated, and older content would need to be archived—all of which I needed to ensure that the client team could accomplish within the scope of the project.

Categorizing content isn't just about the ideal content, but about the time, funding, and staffing of the team responsible for managing that content after launch. Content authors are users, too! It is shortsighted at best (and hostile at worst) to propose content that demands more from the content team than their reality allows.

Be wary of strategies that will require massive amounts of new writing or intensive maintenance—small marketing or communications teams rarely have a steady supply of well-supported writers and managers. You can only flourish within constraints when you acknowledge what those constraints are.

All things considered

By thinking critically about the user needs, business goals, current state of the content, and future goals of the content, I was able to recommend new ways of categorizing the Posse Foundation's content—which led to a new sitemap, new navigation systems, and, eventually, a new site (FIG 3.5).

The new site's top-level categories became:

- **Shaping the Future.** Pages in this section explain the Posse Foundation's mission and the basis for the program; the label is a nod toward their mission to "train these leaders of tomorrow."
- **Recruiting Students.** This category includes content about student eligibility and the process for nominating students to the program.
- **Supporting Scholars.** This category covers details about support resources available, such as a precollegiate training program, on-campus mentorship, and ongoing leadership training.
- **Connecting Alumni.** Pages in this section are focused on career and postgraduate resources, and the Posse Foundation alumni network.

Notice that all of these categories follow the same linguistic pattern—shap*ing*, recruit*ing*, support*ing*, connect*ing*. The parallel structure of the labels underscores the narrative flow between them, while the use of verbs emphasizes user action—without excluding any of their myriad audiences.

FIG 3.5: The new Posse Foundation website organizes content into five categories, seen here in the middle of the page. The design (and language) visually separates the fifth category, Partner with Us, from the four categories that focus on the scholarship life cycle.

There's a fifth category, too: Partner with Us, at the end of the navigation menu, is visually distinct, and uses a different verb structure. It's purposely marked this way to indicate a shift—away from the participles of the previous four categories, and toward a direct address to donors, mentors, and volunteers. The separation both draws attention to the category and reinforces the narrative flow of the other categories.

The process of shaping these categories began by grouping like with like, but didn't end there—if it had, the most important content would have stayed minimized behind a single category. Instead, drawing on the larger design strategy led to a more successful and engaging distribution of content.

CRAFTING LABELS

The content decisions we make, consciously or unconsciously, inherited or created from scratch, dictate value...[For example,] even if we don't especially care whether or not the woman we're reading about is married, we're made acutely aware of

it anyway because the convention [of using "Mrs."] normalizes it, turning it into a reasonable thing to not only want to know, but expect to know.
—Dave Thomas, "The Revolution Will Have Structured Content" (http://bkaprt.com/eia/03-05/)

When we're building categories, the language that we use to label them is just as important as the borders that define them. Sometimes the labels write themselves; other times we struggle with finding the right words; but most of the time, I'd wager, we label our categories with the first thing that comes to mind. If it makes sense, we call it done. After all, who wants to quibble with such tiny details?

Of course, I wouldn't be bringing this up if I weren't about to tell you that *you should quibble with such tiny details*. Labels are language, and language is powerful. Even the tiniest labels have the ability to welcome a user or reject them, to open a door or shut one. Labels articulate the choices made around categorization; they make the boundaries visible.

Labels are rarely applied to categories after they're built. Nor are they set in stone first, with content magically gravitating to their correct designations. Instead, labels grow up in tandem *with* your categories; they're part of your criteria-matching process.

This means that you're testing and tweaking your labels as you're testing and tweaking your categories. Changing a label narrows or broadens the scope of what content can fall under it.

Language versus criteria

In 2018, Pinterest rolled out a feature allowing users to create subcategories within their boards, and I rejoiced because *of course I did*.

Since 2011, I'd been treating Pinterest as my personal cookbook—cataloguing recipes, finding cooking inspiration, and planning meals. But the years—and lack of nested categories—had taken a toll on my boards: what had once been a curated collection of recipes was an overgrown clutter that could only be ordered by pin date (**FIG 3.6**).

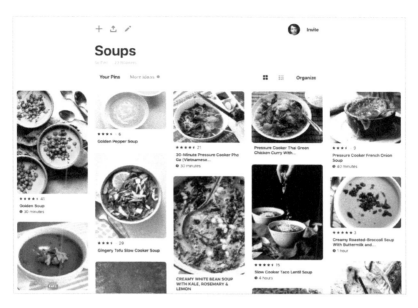

FIG 3.6: My Pinterest system had organized recipes at a high level, like this board for Soups, but finding a specific soup was dependent on remembering how recently I pinned it.

Adding subcategories to my various food boards would make it easier to find a given pin amongst the wilds. But first, I had to sort the pins of each board to determine what those subcategories might be.

I started with the hundred-or-so pins in my Desserts board. I created Cookies as my first subcategory, because cookies were easily identifiable—that is, until I saw a recipe for pistachio blondies. Delicious, but...a cookie? Did it match cookie criteria? I couldn't tell, because I hadn't really defined *cookie*. I just knew, intrinsically, what a cookie was, until I didn't.

Blondies—like a brownie, but using brown sugar instead of cocoa—*could* be considered a cookie, but by that logic, so could brownies. But if I was including brownies, then wouldn't the criteria extend to all bar-shaped confections, like lemon squares? And if I'm including lemon squares, why not custard

Desserts

104 Pins · 7 sections · 27 followers

Your Pins   More ideas ●

Bundts & Tea Cakes

Cakes & Frostings

Cheesecakes

Cookies & Bars

Fruit

Pastries

FIG 3.7: Would apple cake fall under Bundts & Tea Cakes, Cakes & Frostings, or Fruit? Trick question; apple cake is damp bread.

tarts? And if custard tarts, why not cheesecakes? *Why even have subcategories at all?* Oh, this precious house of cards.

My Cookies label became Cookies & Bars to accommodate brownies, blondies, and, yes, lemon squares (I had to draw the line somewhere). Other subcategories followed: I'd take a stab at a label, sort into the label until a recipe defied the criteria, adjust the label, and try again. Eventually, all my pins found a subcategory home (even if I am *still* making changes) (**FIG 3.7**).

Whether you're sorting your private recipe stash or organizing web content, the process is the same: you create a label, you test the label, you tweak the label. You create the criteria, you test the criteria, you tweak the criteria. The criteria and the language work together to determine and declare the category boundaries.

The criteria for my Pinterest boards doesn't have to be apparent to anyone but me; we can disagree about the nature of pastries all day, and it won't matter so long as I—the primary and, likely, only audience—can find my pastelitos recipe. But when working with stakeholder content, how do we ensure that our decision-making makes sense to users?

Guidelines for labels

In some cases, the right label for a category may be quite obvious—a section dedicated to posting news articles may not need much consideration beyond *News*. But in other cases, choosing the right words can be challenging. There are four qualities I try to prioritize in my labels:

- Clarity
- Specificity
- Inclusivity
- Consistency

Writing microcopy (small bits of language used in interface design) is an art unto itself, but if you don't have a copywriter on your team, steering into these qualities can keep you on the right track. Let's break them down a bit.

Clarity

Users appreciate straightforward labels with familiar language, free of confusion and ambiguity. Your user research can help: look for the words (especially the verbs!) that people use when interacting with your site or product, then mirror their language back to them. Category labels and navigation structures are not the place to socialize corporate lingo or experiment with affordances (**FIG 3.8**). Creativity is wonderful, but not at the expense of clear, accurate communication.

Clear, of course, doesn't have to mean dull. Don't automatically accept the most obvious label that pops into your head—push back and explore further. There's an opportunity to express the design strategy in these tiny details, as we've already

FIG 3.8: Twitter's "Moments" label required considerable marketing to help users understand it when it was first introduced. I...still don't understand it.

seen with the Posse Foundation. Remember, language is a rich tapestry—it's possible to be clear and accurate while also conveying your brand, story, and values.

Specificity

Avoid, at all costs, miscellaneous or catch-all categories with generalized labels (**FIG 3.9**). These sometimes show up when there are larger classification problems on the site, leading to a handful of items that don't seem to fit anywhere in particular (http://bkaprt.com/eia/03-06/). They can also appear when the labels simply aren't specific enough to accurately describe the contents. Like all junk drawers, these categories will clutter up with pen caps, broken rubber bands, and disconnected content, leading users to ignore or avoid them.

Inclusivity

Don't alienate your users! That's obvious, but we too often forget the sparkling variety of who we mean: users on mobile devices, users reading with assistive technology, users in high-stress situations, users with low literacy, users with temporary impairments, users from marginalized communities, users with drastically different perspectives, lives, and expectations from our own—so, you know, *all* of them.

We are often well-intentioned, but *impact* matters more than *intent*—so be purposeful about inclusivity. Get input from diverse groups of users and colleagues. Ask yourself: How might these labels be misconstrued or harmful? How can I use this language to reduce harm, or to make space for more people (**FIG 3.10**)?

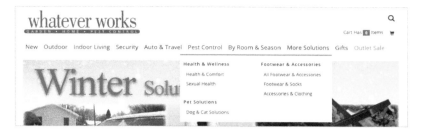

FIG 3.9: This makes me want to push my computer into the sea.

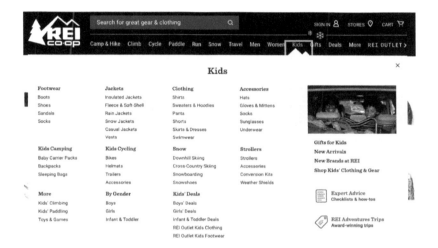

FIG 3.10: The REI website labels its kids' subcategories by type and by sport, deprioritizing categorization by gender—a welcome difference from clothing websites that push gender divisions (and stereotypes).

Consistency

Try to use similar language, syntax, or parts of speech for labels that will be read in a group—for instance, use all verbs, all gerunds, or all nouns. Consistency can speed up understanding and create appealing linguistic rhythm (**FIG 3.11**). But beware—consistent language doesn't always lead to consistent meaning, and meaning is *much* more important (**FIG 3.12**).

FIG 3.11: The gerunds in mass.gov's main navigation create consistent sound—and expectations. The change in the fifth category could indicate a change in purpose.

FIG 3.12: Comcast went for consistency at the expense of meaning. Products will show me products I can have; Bundles & Deals will show me bundles and deals I can have; Programming will show me programming I can have; so, obviously, Customers must show me customers I can have?

Watch your first- and second-person possessive pronouns ("my" and "your"). For example, About Us and My Account both use first-person point of view, even though, in this case, *Us* refers to the company and *My* refers to the user. In *Conversational Design*, Erika Hall explained the rules for this quite nicely:

> *Things belonging to the company that created the system, such as a feature or privacy policy, are "ours." Things belonging to the user, such as a profile or shopping cart, are "yours." Anything that's just part of the overall experience doesn't necessarily need a possessive pronoun at all.*

That last sentence gets overlooked all too often (**FIG 3.13**).

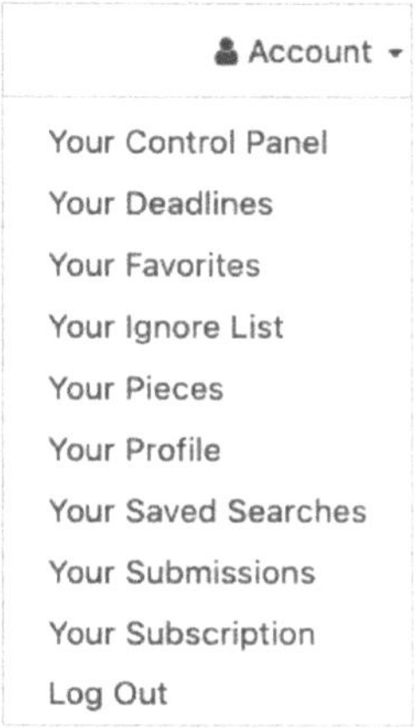

👤 Account ▾

Your Control Panel

Your Deadlines

Your Favorites

Your Ignore List

Your Pieces

Your Profile

Your Saved Searches

Your Submissions

Your Subscription

Log Out

FIG 3.13: Calm down, Duotrope.

THE POWER OF CATEGORIZATION

Categorizing and labeling content is an alchemical process that—when it works well—results in clear, user-centered, strategically defined structures. These structures can become the conceptual backbone of the entire site experience.

Of course, when categories are created thoughtlessly or in bad faith, they can be destructive, as we saw with Walter Plecker at the beginning of this book. "Categories are both powerful and fundamentally arbitrary," information architect Sarah R. Barrett rightly tweeted in 2017, "which is a dangerous combination" (http://bkaprt.com/eia/03-07/).

Ultimately, categorization *is* subjective, just as many of our design decisions are—but we can try to reduce arbitrariness through research, inclusivity, and respect for our users. When we consider the impact—not just the intentions—behind our categorical choices, we are more likely to build systems that work for real people.

And speaking of systems: if all this talk of categories has you feeling like we're halfway to a sitemap already, well, that's because we are. The work of categorical criteria and labels lays a foundation for the structure of the site. Our next step is to document the system.

4 SITE STRUCTURE

PROJECT 100 HAD A SIMPLE GOAL: to see one hundred progressive women serving in Congress by 2020. To get there, its founders built a website (project100.org) to showcase the positions and values of every progressive woman running for office.

And with a record number of women running for office in 2018, Project 100 had no shortage of content challenges. Condensing nuanced platform details for each candidate to just a few bullet points was difficult enough—but they still needed to be arranged on the site in a clear, balanced way.

Project 100 cofounder Eduardo Ortiz started first with an algorithm to elevate "trending" candidates, enabling those with strong name recognition to appear at the top of the page. However, Ortiz said, "we wanted people to understand that there are more qualified candidates than the ones who make it to the mainstream or get reported by the media." To keep lesser-known candidates from disappearing behind a curtain, he designed without pagination:

If we were to paginate the candidates, those who have fewer resources would be displayed on later pages, continuing that disparity...Paginating would have been an arbitrary decision for organizing the candidates. Not paginating was an idealistic approach to giving everyone a level playing field.

This simple but well-considered design decision ensured that all candidates could easily be brought to users' attention. (Coincidentally, the 2018 elections met Project 100's goal two years early. Maybe it was the information architecture, maybe it was the power of democracy.)

Pagination would have changed the way candidate information could be discovered and understood—as well as the structure of the site. The meaning and impact of the content tells us not only how to display it, categorize it, and label it, but also how to connect it into a functional, overarching system.

AUDITING FOR STRUCTURE

Just as we need to understand our content before we can recategorize it, we need to understand the system before we try to rebuild it.

Enter the structural audit: a review of the site focused solely on its menus, links, flows, and hierarchies. I know you thought we were done with audits back in Chapter 2, but hear me out! Structural audits have an important and singular purpose: to help us build a new sitemap.

This isn't about recreating the *intended* sitemap—no, this is about experiencing the site the way users experience it. This audit is meant to track and record the structure of the site as it *really* works.

Setting up the template

First, we're gonna need another spreadsheet. (Look, it is not *my* fault that spreadsheets are the perfect system for recording audit data. I don't make the rules.)

	A	B
1	**Page ID**	**URL**
2	**1.0**	First level
3	1.1	Second level
4	1.1.1	Third level
5	1.1.1.1	Fourth level
6	1.1.1.1.1	Fifth Level
7	1.1.1.1.1.1	Sixth Level
8		On-page navigation
9		External link
10		File
11		**Unknown hierarchy**
12		**Crosslink**

FIG 4.1: I use a color-coded outline key to record page hierarchy as I move through the audit. Wait, how many circles did Dante write about?

Because this involves building a spreadsheet from scratch, I keep a "template" at the top of my audit files—rows that I can copy and paste into each new audit (FIG 4.1). It's a color-coded outline key that helps me track my page hierarchy *and* my place in the auditing process. When auditing thousands of pages, it's easy to get dizzyingly lost, particularly when coming back into the sheet after a break; the key helps me stay oriented, no matter how deep the rabbit hole.

Color-coding

Color is the easiest, quickest way to convey page depth at a glance. The repetition of black text, white cells, and gray lines can have a numbing effect—too many rows of sameness, and your eyes glaze over. My coloring may result in a spreadsheet that looks like a twee box of macarons, but at least I know, instantly, where I am.

The exact colors don't really matter, but I find that the familiar mental model of a rainbow helps with recognition—the cooler the row color, the deeper into the site I know I must be.

The nested rainbow of pages is great when you're auditing neatly nested pages—but most websites color outside the lines (pun *extremely* intended) with their structure. I leave my orderly rainbow behind to capture duplicate pages, circular links, external navigation, and other inconsistencies like:

- **On-page navigation.** A bright text color denotes pages that are accessible via links within page content—not through the navigation. These pages are critical to site structure but are easily overlooked. Not every page *needs* to be displayed in the navigation menus, of course—news articles are a perfect example—but sometimes this indicates publishing errors.
- **External links.** These are navigation links that go to pages outside the domain. They might be social media pages, or even sites held by the same company—but if the domain isn't the one I'm auditing, I don't need to follow it. I *do* need to note its existence in my spreadsheet, so I color the text as the red flag that it is. (As a *general* rule, I steer clients away from placing external links in navigation, in order to maintain a consistent experience. If there's a need to send users offsite, I'll suggest using a contextual, on-page link.)
- **Files.** This mostly refers to PDFs, but can include Word files, slide decks, or anything else that requires downloading. As with external links, I want to capture anything that might disrupt the in-site browsing experience. (My audits usually filter out PDFs, but for organizations that overuse them, I'll audit them separately to show how much "website" content is locked inside.)
- **Unknown hierarchy.** Every once in a while, there's a page that doesn't seem to belong anywhere—maybe it's missing from the menu, while its URL suggests it belongs in one section and its navigation scheme suggests another. These pages need to be discussed with their owners to determine whether the content needs to be considered in the new site.
- **Crosslinks.** These are navigation links for pages that canonically live in a different section of the site—in other words, they're duplicates. This often happens in footer navigation, which may repeat the main navigation or surface links to deeper-but-important pages (like a Contact page or a privacy

policy). I don't want to record the same information about the page twice, but I do need to know where the crosslink is, so I can track different paths to the content. I color these cells gray so they don't draw my attention.

Note that coloring every row (and indenting, as you'll see in a moment) can be a tedious process—unless you rely on Excel's formatting brush. That tool applies all the right styles in just two quick clicks.

Outlines and page IDs

Color-coding is half of my template; the other half is the outline, which is how I keep track of the structure itself. (No big deal, just *the entire point of the spreadsheet*.)

Every page in the site gets assigned an ID. *You* are assigning this number; it doesn't correspond to anything but your own perception of the navigation. This number does three things for you:

1. It associates pages with their place in the site hierarchy. Decimals indicate levels, so the page ID can be decoded as the page's place in the system.
2. It gives each page a unique identifier, so you can easily refer to a particular page—saying "2.4.1" is much clearer than "you know that one page in the fourth product category?"
3. You can keep using the ID in other contexts, like your sitemap. Then, later, when your team decides to wireframe pages 1.1.1 and 7.0, you'll all be working from the same understanding.

Let me be completely honest: things might get goofy sometimes with the decimal outline. There will come a day when you'll find yourself casually typing out "1.2.1.2.1.1.1," and at that moment, a fellow auditor somewhere in the universe will ring a tiny gong for you.

In addition to the IDs, I indent each level, which reinforces both the numbers and the colors. Each level down—each digit in the ID, each change in color—gets one indentation.

I identify top-level pages with a single number: 1.0, 2.0, 3.0, etc. The next page level in the first section would be 1.1, 1.2, 1.3, and so on. I mark the homepage as 0.0, which is mildly controversial—the homepage is technically a level above—but, look: I've got a lot of numbers to write, and I don't need those numbers to tell me they're under the homepage, so this is my system. Feel free to use the numbering system that work best for you.

Criteria and columns

So we've got some secret codes for tracking hierarchy and depth, but what about other structural criteria? What are our spreadsheet *columns* (**FIG 4.2**)? In addition to a column for Page ID, here's what I cover:

- **URL.** I don't consistently fill out this column, because I already collected this data back in my automated audit. I include it every twenty entries or so (and on crosslinks or pages with unknown hierarchy) as another way of tracking progress, and as a direct link into the site itself.
- **Menu label/link.** I include this column only if I notice a lot of mismatches between links, labels, and page names. Perfect agreement isn't required; but frequent, significant differences between the language that *leads* to a page and the language *on the page itself* may indicate inconsistencies in editorial approach or backend structures.
- **Name/headline.** Think of this as "what does the page owner call it?" It may be the H1, or an H2; it may match the link that brought you here, or the page title in the browser, or it may not.
- **Page title.** This is for the name of the page in the metadata. Again, I don't use this in every audit—particularly if the site uses the same long, branded metadata title for every single page—but frequent mismatches can be useful to track.
- **Section.** While the template can indicate your level, it can't tell you which area of the site you're in—unless you write it down. (This may differ from the section data you applied to your automated audit, taken from the URL structure; here, you're noting the section where the page appears.)

	Page ID	URL	Menu label/link	Name/headline	Page title	Section	Notes
2	1.0	First level					
3	1.1	Second level					
4	1.1.1	Third level					
5	1.1.1.1	Fourth level					
6	1.1.1.1.1	Fifth Level					
7	1.1.1.1.1.1	Sixth Level					
8		On-page navigation					
9		External link					
10		File					
11		Unknown hierarchy					
12		Crosslink					
13	0.0	http://www.gettysburg.edu/	Gettysburg College	Gettysburg College	Gettysburg College - liberal arts & sciences college in Gettysburg, PA		
14	1.0	http://www.gettysburg.edu/about/	About	About the College	About the College	About	
15	1.1	https://www.gettysburg.edu/about/photo_ga	Photos & Videos	Photos & Videos	Gettysburg College - Photos & Videos	About	Inconsistent page links throug
16	1.1.1	https://www.gettysburg.edu/about/videos/in	Watch videos from around campus	Videos		About	
17	1.1.2	https://www.gettysburg.edu/about/photo_ga	Campus Buildings	Campus Buildings		About	
18	1.1.3	https://www.gettysburg.edu/about/photo_ga	Athletics	Athletics		About	
19	1.1.3.1	https://www.gettysburg.edu/about/photo_ga	View athletic facilities	Athletic Facilities		About	
20	1.1.4	https://www.gettysburg.edu/about/photo_ga	Seasons	Seasons		About	
21	1.1.5	https://www.gettysburg.edu/about/photo_ga	Campus Life	Campus Life		About	
22	1.1.6	https://www.gettysburg.edu/about/photo_ga	Classrooms & Labs	Classrooms & Labs		About	
23	1.1.7	https://www.gettysburg.edu/about/photo_ga	Housing & Dining	Housing & Dining		About	
24	1.1.8	https://www.gettysburg.edu/about/photo_ga	Fine & Performing Arts	Fine & Performing Arts		About	
25	1.1.9	https://www.gettysburg.edu/virtual-tour/inde	Explore the Virtual Tour	Virtual Tour		Other	Feels like a microsite or iframe
26	1.2	http://www.gettysburg.edu/news_events/	News@Gettysburg	News@Gettysburg			
27	1.3	http://www.gettysburg.edu/facts_figures/ind	Facts & Figures	Facts & Figures		About	
28	1.3.1	http://www.gettysburg.edu/facts_figures/gla	Gettysburg at a glance	At a glance		About	
29	1.3.2	http://www.gettysburg.edu/facts_figures/aca	Academic program	Academic program		About	
30	1.3.3	http://www.gettysburg.edu/facts_figures/det	High-Impact Practices	Participation in High-Impact Learning Experiences		About	
31	1.3.4	http://www.gettysburg.edu/facts_figures/fac	Faculty	Faculty		About	
32	1.3.5	http://www.gettysburg.edu/facts_figures/ret	Retention & graduation rates	Retention & graduation rates		About	

FIG 4.2: A semi-complete structural audit. This view shows a lot of second- and third-level pages, as well as pages accessed through on-page navigation.

- **Notes.** Finally, I keep a column to note specific challenges, and to track patterns I'm seeing across multiple pages—things like "Different template, missing subnav" or "Only visible from previous page." My only caution here is that if you're planning to share this audit with another person, make sure your notes are—*ahem*—professional. Unless you enjoy anxiously combing through hundreds of entries to revise comments like "Wow haha nope" (not that I would know anything about that).

Depending on your project needs, there may be other columns, too. If, in addition to using this spreadsheet for your new sitemap, you want to use it in migration planning or template mapping, you may want columns for new URLs, or template types.

You can get your own copy of my template as a downloadable Excel file (http://bkaprt.com/eia/04-01/, XLSX). Feel free to tweak it to suit your style and needs; I know I always do. As long as your spreadsheet helps you understand the hierarchy and structure of your website, you're good to go.

Gathering data

Setting up the template is one thing—actually filling it out is, admittedly, another. So how do we go from a shiny, new, naive spreadsheet to a complete, jaded, seen-some-*stuff* spreadsheet? I always liked Erin Kissane's description of the process, from *The Elements of Content Strategy*:

> Big inventories involve a lot of black coffee, a few late nights, and a playlist of questionable but cheering music prominently featuring the soundtrack of object-collecting video game Katamari Damacy. It takes quite a while to exhaustively inventory a large site, but it's the only way to really understand what you have to work with.

We're not talking about the same kind of exhaustive inventory she was describing (though I *am* recommending Katamari music). But even our less intensive approach is going to require your butt in a seat, your eyes on a screen, and a certain amount of patience and focus. You're about to walk, with your fingers, through most of a website.

Start on the homepage. (We know that not all users start there, but we've got to have some kind of order to this process or we'll never get through it.) Explore the main navigation before moving on to secondary navigation structures. Move left to right, top to bottom (assuming that is your language direction) over each page, looking for the links. You want to record every page you can reasonably access on the site, noting navigational and structural considerations as you go.

My advice as you work:

· **Use two monitors.** I struggle immensely without two screens in this process, which involves constantly switching between spreadsheet and browser in rapid, tennis-match-like succession. If you don't have access to multiple monitors, find whatever way is easiest for you to quickly flip between applications.

- **Record what you see.** I generally note all visible menu links at the same level, then exhaust one section at a time. Sometimes this means I have to adjust what I initially observed, or backtrack to pages I missed earlier. You might prefer to record all data across a level before going deeper, and that would work, too. Just be consistent to minimize missed links.
- **Be alert to inconsistencies.** On-page links, external links, and crosslinks can tell you a lot about the structure of the site, but they're easy to overlook. Missed on-page links mean missed content; missed crosslinks mean duplicate work. (Note: the further you get into the site, the more you'll start seeing crosslinks, given all the pages you've already recorded.)
- **Stick to what's structurally relevant.** A single file that's not part of a larger pattern of file use is not going to change your understanding of the structure. Neither is recording every single blog post, quarterly newsletter, or news story in the archive. For content that's dynamic, repeatable, and plentiful, I use an x in the page ID to denote more of the same. For example, a news archive with a page ID of 2.8 might show just one entry beneath it as 2.8.x; I don't need to record every page up to 2.8.791 to understand that there are 791 articles on the site (assuming I noted that fact in an earlier content review).
- **Save.** Save *frequently*. I cannot even begin to speak of the unfathomable heartbreak that is Microsoft Excel burning an unsaved audit to the ground.

Knowing which links to follow, which to record, and how best to untangle structural confusion—that improves with time and experience. Performing structural audits will not only teach you about your current site, but will help you develop fluency in systems thinking—a boon when it comes time to document the new site.

BUILDING SITEMAPS

The structural audit paints a picture of how the current system is put together, which should inform your new system. You don't want to replicate it—you want to understand its weaknesses, so you don't recreate them; and understand its strengths, so you don't leave them behind. You've learned how the current pages work together experientially; now you can dream up more effective page relationships across the site.

Your sitemap is where you document the dreaming. It's an artifact for communicating the *hierarchy* of pages in your site. It records your categories and labels, and maps out how content on the new site will be organized within them. It is your system's north star.

The value of sitemaps

First, let's consider the direct relationships to be documented: parent-child relationships between pages at different levels in the hierarchy, and sibling relationships between pages at the same level in the hierarchy (**FIG 4.3**).

"But," you might be saying, "my web pages have much more complicated connections, well beyond parent-child and sibling relationships!" Well—good! I would hope your site provides *plenty* of fluid paths for users to find the content they need as quickly as possible. But sitemaps are not meant to capture *every* possible path; indirect relationships between pages, and creative ways of surfacing content, won't necessarily appear here.

Even if you're not thinking in a strictly page-like way about your designs—I know, I know, we've broken the boundaries of the *page*, and we're supposed to be designing *experiences*, not boxes—there are still plenty of benefits to articulating the structure of your site through a sitemap:

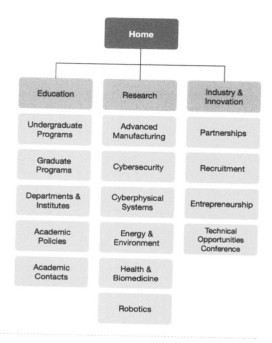

FIG 4.3: This sample from a sitemap for Carnegie Mellon University's College of Engineering shows two levels of hierarchy—landing pages presented horizontally across the top, and their child pages presented vertically underneath.

- **Shared vocabulary.** Sitemaps are an opportunity to rally around common terminology. When you have to speak in the abstract about pages that don't even exist yet, and you have to do that with designers and developers and copywriters and marketers and project managers and stakeholders, you'll be glad to have a document that codifies page titles or ID numbers (as in the structural audit).
- **Complete inventory.** Similarly, you need a place to keep a complete list of *the stuff*—the pages in the new site, or, if you're living the post-page dream, the collections of screens or other content displays. (I'm gonna call this "pages" for short, fight me.) Eventually you'll need to know, say, which pages will appear in a local navigation menu so you can design said menu. A complete inventory for the site will come in handy more than once during design and development.

- **Mapped hierarchy.** Even if all a sitemap can capture is parent-child and sibling relationships, that's quite a lot—and if you're not capturing that data here, where else would you do it? Understanding the hierarchy of pages means you have a baseline for the potential paths users *could* take through the system—a starting point for mapping user journeys or customer touchpoints.

Admittedly, I'm subtweeting a bit to all the times I've heard someone say, "But do we really *need* a sitemap?" But the way a site is put together is a design choice, and documentation helps us conceptualize and communicate our choices.

The sitemap is an artifact—it needs to be articulated textually or visually (or both), not only to record your structural decisions, but to share the context for your work with colleagues and stakeholders.

Documentation styles

The best documentation is the one that works for you, so consider how the sitemap can assist with the next steps in your project. Will it be used to garner stakeholder approval? To demonstrate progress in the project plan? To prepare for a CMS migration? To identify pages for wireframing?

All of those are valid uses for a sitemap (and your sitemap may meet multiple needs at once). But different styles of documentation have different levels of detail, and so are suited for different purposes.

Box-and-arrow diagrams

When people (especially stakeholders) hear "sitemap," they often think of a visual diagram: a series of boxes arranged in a tree-like structure, connected by lines denoting hierarchy (**FIG 4.4**).

This visual approach is excellent for presenting high-level structure, particularly to stakeholders who don't want to get caught up in details. On the flip side, because these diagrams don't have much room for detail, they tend to work best for smaller sites, or overviews of larger sites.

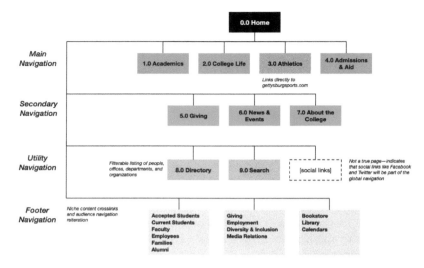

FIG 4.4: A box-and-arrow sitemap for Gettysburg College, showing the top level of each navigational structure.

My sitemap diagrams span multiple pages: first, a page that shows *all* navigation structures, one level deep (**FIG 4.4**), then subsequent pages that show the details within each navigation structure (**FIG 4.5**). (If I find that this isn't enough to convey the structure, that's an indication that I should try a text-based sitemap format instead.)

Visually, sitemap diagrams are entirely up to you. Some people prefer horizontal arrangements to vertical ones; some avoid color. Colors, connectors, borders, shading—it's your call. Just make sure whatever signifiers you apply to your diagram contribute meaningful information. This is particularly important when sharing the sitemap with others; consider including a legend if your system isn't readily apparent to those who need to approve or act on it.

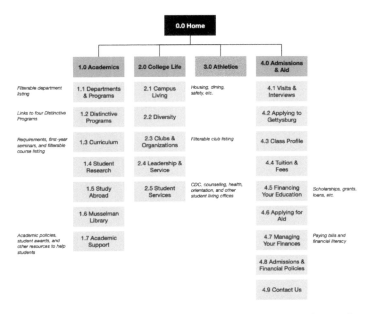

FIG 4.5: The second page of the same Gettysburg College sitemap, showing the second level of the main navigation.

Outlines

For a more textual approach, try an outline—yep, just a plain ol' outline, in a plain ol' document (**FIG 4.6**). Outlines are the epitome of hierarchical documentation—that's literally why they exist—so you can see how that format works nicely for recording a hierarchy of pages.

Outlines are a good choice for completionist scenarios. If you need to show *every* page at *every* level, across multiple nested levels, an outline is a much more effective record than a box-and-arrow diagram.

On the other hand, outlines can become quite long, text-heavy, and wavy with indentations and decimals. Stakeholders who were expecting an easy-on-the-eyes diagram may not interpret this as a "sitemap"—so, once again, consider the needs of your project at this stage.

```
Primary

0.0  Home
1.0  Academics
     1.1  Areas of Study
          1.1.1    Business
          1.1.2    Education
          1.1.3    Language, Culture & Communication
          1.1.4    Political Science & Law
          1.1.5    Theology & Philosophy
          1.1.6    Science & Engineering
          1.1.7    Health Sciences
          1.1.8    Social Sciences
          1.1.9    Visual Arts
          1.1.10   Performing Arts
     1.2  Undergraduate Programs
          1.2.1    [Programs]
                   1.2.1.1  Degrees
                   1.2.1.2  [Facilities/Internships/Residencies/etc.]
                   1.2.1.3  Meet the Faculty
                   1.2.1.4  Career Opportunities
     1.3  Graduate Programs
          1.3.1    [Programs]
                   1.3.1.1  Degrees
                   1.3.1.2  [Facilities/Internships/Residencies/etc.]
                   1.3.1.3  Meet the Faculty
```

FIG 4.6: An example of a sitemap outline.

Spreadsheets

If you need to record more than *just* page hierarchy, you'll need to turn to our friend the spreadsheet (again: not my fault). Much like our structural audit, a sitemap spreadsheet creates room for a wealth of data—such as identifying each page's source content, new URL strategies, content revision status, page ownership, deadlines associated with migration, and more (FIG 4.7).

If you conducted a structural audit, you're ahead of the game here: you can use that spreadsheet as a springboard for the new sitemap. (Save a copy!) It's an excellent way to track the progression of content from the old site to the new.

It's also ideal for collaborating on wireframing, templating, migration, and other development efforts, which may need more metadata than a diagram or outline can provide.

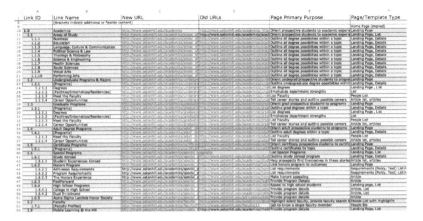

FIG 4.7: This sitemap was based on the spreadsheet of a structural audit, adding columns for new URLs, source URLs, the purpose of each page, and the intended design template.

Filling in the details

Depending on the format you use for your sitemap documentation, you'll need to include different kinds of data and different levels of granularity. But, generally speaking, these are my recommendations for building a well-documented sitemap:

- **Use consistent page identification.** If you created page IDs in a structural audit, keep that system going—the numbers likely won't match perfectly because of changes in content, but the consistency can keep project teammates oriented. If you didn't use page IDs before, start now.
- **Differentiate between single pages and collections.** For site sections that continuously generate new content of the same content type—like events, blog posts, and articles—indicate that plurality as succinctly as possible. In a visual sitemap, I might overlap several boxes to suggest multiple pages; in a text-based sitemap, I might write the page type in brackets, rather than an individual title (e.g. "[News articles]").
- **Don't forget outliers.** It's tempting to think you only need to document new content, or significant pages, or just the

main navigation—but that wouldn't be a complete picture of the structure. Refer back to the notes you took during the structural audit, and make sure your sitemap reflects all the necessary navigation structures, components, and pages that will truly make up the site.

- **Aim for editorial accuracy.** When possible, try to use the spellings, punctuation, capitalization, character lengths, and other style considerations preferred by the content owners (especially if there are branded terms or stakeholder concerns about language). Check in with writers or marketers who might know about editorial guidelines; even small mistakes in labels can ruffle feathers and lead to slowdowns in approval.
- **Add context.** If you're hoping your sitemap will garner buy-in from stakeholders, you might need to provide rationale that isn't part of the sitemap itself—perhaps through a report, a slide deck, or document annotations. You might need to explain what content each page will contain, where different links might appear, which content areas have been added or removed, or any other changes that aren't self-evident or might take stakeholders by surprise.

If you've made it this far, then congratulations: you've got a sitemap (plus my respect and admiration)!

But—no matter how rigorous your decision-making, how justified your choices, how solid your data—you're probably about to make some changes.

MAKING ADJUSTMENTS

Maybe you've received feedback from stakeholders. Maybe you've been told about unexpected content changes that undermine your category labels (oops). Maybe you've done some testing (see the Resources section), and users seem confused by your language. Or maybe you're still iterating, and the sitemap just hasn't gelled yet.

Whatever your situation, there comes a point (er, probably multiple points) where you'll have to revise your site structure. Revisions are usually motivated by one of two things: purity (i.e. the structure doesn't feel balanced, clear, consistent, etc.) or politics (i.e. a stakeholder's favorite page is buried, a label doesn't sound *important* enough, etc.).

When adjusting the sitemap (whether to please your stakeholders or yourself), you have a few levers to manipulate:

- **Change the labels.** Labels, as we've seen, limit your criteria and the content that matches. Review your earlier language decisions and the inputs that led to them. Sometimes, a simple tweak to the wording is all that's needed; other times, labels need to be entirely rewritten, altering the collection of pages within them.
- **Change the categories.** Same idea from a different angle: reexamine the distribution of content. Try out alternative ways of grouping the content, and see how they open up new ways of thinking, different expressions of the strategy, or reworded labels.
- **Change the content.** In some cases (especially if your content analysis was on the lighter side), the content itself may be leading you astray. You might need to turn long pages into multiple shorter ones, or add information to an underdeveloped section, or even delete or add content. Be careful, though—don't change the content just to make the sitemap fit an ideal. Just be willing to consider how potential changes to the copy might benefit the structure (and, *ahem*, the user).
- **Rethink your approach.** As a last resort, you might want to start from scratch—not to throw away all your hard work, but to eliminate any baggage that's accumulated through the process (*cough* internal politics *cough*) and find a new perspective on the structure. Sometimes we make assumptions early in the process that don't necessarily serve us in the end.

I wish I could give you a formula to follow—some tried-and-true equation where x + y = a scientifically correct sitemap, one so airtight that all content is perfectly exposed and no stakeholder can question the category labels.

But this practice is closer to art than science. We blend a little bit of instinct, a little bit of nerves, and as much data as we can gather to make decisions. No site launches with a perfect sitemap; no sitemap is free from politics and biases and rushed timelines.

The sitemap is the heart and soul of your site structure. But it's also just one artifact—and a limited one, at that. To ensure a usable structure, we must also illuminate the paths through our content, and help users stay oriented on their journey, wherever it may take them.

5 NAVIGATION AND WAYFINDING

WEBSITES ARE ALL ALIKE, IN SOME WAYS. The internet's been around long enough now that—whatever carousels and tables and JavaScript frameworks come and go—we've developed certain expectations about how websites function.

We have, collectively, a mental map for website organization. We expect navigation somewhere near the top of the page. We expect some kind of footer. We generally look for subnavigation in dropdowns or to the sides.

Building off those shared expectations supports information access. When we encounter systems that buck convention (oooh, how *disruptive* and *edgy*), we often can't use the information as effectively or efficiently as we can in a system that matches our mental model.

That's not meant to squash our creativity or condemn us to sites made out of ticky-tacky. It just means we need to be respectful of how far we can push that particular Overton window. It's a point of admiration, too: look at how quickly, in the oh-so-short history of the web, we've been able to establish effective affordances!

A large part of organizing information online is organizing for findability and access. Cutting-edge categorization and slick sitemaps don't mean much if the content can't be found and used—which is why tools and tricks that promise to deliver the *precisely* right content to the *precisely* right eyeballs at the *precisely* right times are so seductive. But before you start reaching for magic wands, remember that findability and access start here: with clear, well-structured content arranged in clear, well-structured ways.

Now that we've determined the best arrangement of pages, we have to dig into how our users move through them. What paths can they take? How do they keep track of where they are? How do they know where to go next? How can we ensure that they arrive at their intended destinations, safe and sound?

PLOTTING THE COURSE

When we make a sitemap, we're documenting the skeleton of the site: how the pages are put together, how the content is categorized, and how we expect our users to weave their way through it.

Of course, we know our users will take whatever paths they please, which may or may not dovetail with our expectations. But the navigation structures of a website are a starting point: they offer at last one potential path in to the content.

If navigation were simply a table of contents, we would, quite reasonably, design it that way. But navigation is much more than an index of topics—it creates meaning. How much the navigation reveals, what it chooses to prioritize, and how the paths are labeled can tell users *everything* about the content (and the people behind it).

This is why we must be just as deliberate with our navigation structures as we are about any other aspect of the design. We must ensure that we're providing our users with clear, accessible, established pathways into the content.

Navigation structures

I identify *navigation structures* as any conceptually unique interface that provides access to deeper content. The structures I generally work with include:

- **Main navigation.** Sometimes called primary or global navigation, this is exactly what it sounds like: the key navigation structure that accesses your most important content. When you're categorizing and labeling content, you're usually doing so with this "main menu" in mind.
- **Secondary navigation.** Again, exactly what it sounds like—navigation to content that's considered secondary to the core content. In many of the sites I work on, secondary navigations tend to hold institutional or operational content that plays a supporting role in the site's purpose, like About Us or News pages.
- **Utility navigation.** This often contains functionality like portals, logins, account access, shopping carts, directories, and sometimes the search bar and social navigation. Not every site needs it; in many sites, the secondary and utility navigation are the same.
- **Search.** While the search bar is sometimes considered part of other navigation structures, it can be useful to call attention to it separately in documentation. It's a critical element, yet so fundamental that it can get overlooked as a structural component. (You remembered to include it—and the results page—in your sitemap, right?)
- **Social navigation.** While a series of social icons isn't, strictly speaking, "navigation" (picky, picky!), it's important to be aware of major links that will direct visitors away from the domain. Social accounts, blogs, partner sites, and any other requisite links to a company's digital ecosystem need to be documented *somewhere*—and you might as well do it in the navigation.
- **Header or footer navigation.** Headers and footers usually refer to the areas at the top and bottom of a page (assuming there is a bottom! Endless scrolling doesn't offer the most structured experience). Header areas usually hold the sec-

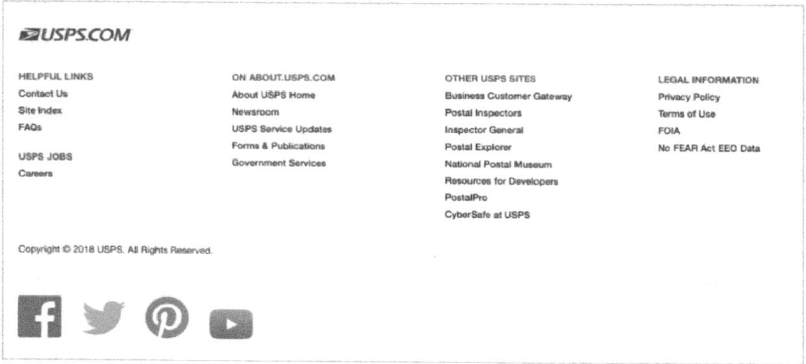

FIG 5.1: The United States Postal Service website footer includes social navigation, links to other domains in its system, and surfaced links to legal policies.

ondary or utility navigation, but they sometimes have their own unique navigation structures. Footers tend to either repeat the main navigation along with the first level of child pages, or display a curated list of interior pages (often chosen to satisfy stakeholder requests for more prominence). In either case, footers can be a way of exposing more content without distracting from the page layout or more central pathways (**FIG 5.1**).

As you can see, these definitions are subjective, and I'm blurring the lines between the structural and visual aspects of navigation. But ultimately, it doesn't matter if you think of the search bar as part of the header navigation, or if you place the social links in a unique interface. What matters is that you document your navigation structures—and start to consider all the other paths users might take to find content.

Too much, too soon

Several years ago, I worked with Seven Heads Design to redesign the website for Seton Hill University. We knew (from our user and stakeholder interviews) that the job of the web-

FIG 5.2: The Seton Hill University homepage was cheerful, but a surplus of navigation structures competed with each other for user attention.

site—like many in higher education—was to attract prospective students.

The homepage at that time offered several different ways to access deeper content (**FIG 5.2**): an eight-item main navigation, a seven-item secondary navigation, a three-item carousel, a dropdown audience selector, a dual-focus search bar, four tabs for events, and four tabs for campus news.

There were so many paths to content, in fact, that most users didn't know which to take. Prospective students felt particularly lost, since the most prominent content and links were for things like campus events, donation requests, and system logins—content intended for current students and alumni.

By surfacing as much content as possible to as many audiences as possible, the navigation structures were backfiring. The target audience was giving up.

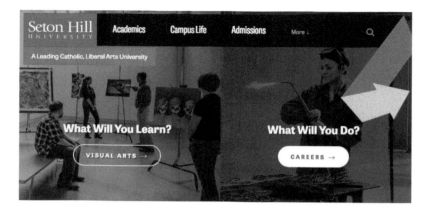

FIG 5.3: The redesigned Seton Hill University homepage, with just a single menu, a detailed dropdown option, and two calls to action (which randomized upon page load, along with the images).

One of our first goals was to redesign the paths to content. We narrowed down the main navigation to just a few menu items: Academics, Campus Life, and Admissions (**FIG 5.3**). These three labels suggested a chronological journey for prospective students to get to know Seton Hill: first, they could learn about educational opportunities; then about the social and extracurricular experiences; and, finally—when they were confident that Seton Hill was a good fit for them—they could investigate the application process.

The rest of the design followed suit with a before-and-after concept that spoke directly to the educational and professional journeys of would-be students. The new look, combined with significantly fewer paths in to the content (counterintuitive as that could seem!), resulted in a much more effective, tailored site.

A few months after the new design launched, we checked the analytics: sessions on the Undergraduate Admissions landing page had more than doubled, and the number of new users was up 185%. Those changes weren't solely the result of our simplified navigation, but certainly more prospective students found their way *in*.

Balanced pathways

One lesson to take from the Seton Hill redesign is that less is more—as long as it's not *too* much less. For every website flooded with menus, there's a website withholding its content. For every rule about web work, we will stumble across an exception. (Even my permaban on FAQs gets lifted in very special circumstances.) (Not yours.)

When we think about paths in to deeper content, there is—as in so many elements of our work—a careful balance to be struck:

- **Too many paths will create indecision...**Choice paralysis is hardly the desired reaction. Trying to put every single possibility in front of every single user every single time is a recipe for disaster. Fewer paths mean quicker decision-making.
- **...and too few paths will create dead ends.** The pendulum can also swing too far in the other direction: if we don't offer *enough* choices, users have nowhere to go. Missing calls to action, poor content visibility, menus that don't connect— all of these end with the user closing the tab or hitting the back button.
- **Establish firm paths...**As we've just seen with Seton Hill, we have to make tough decisions about who and what to prioritize—otherwise, our paths become muddled. The more confident you are about creating clear entry points into the content, the more confident users will be about following them.
- **...but be prepared for users to carve their own.** We know users rarely follow our carefully planned navigation. But when they stray from our journey maps, that shouldn't mean they're lost forever—our information structures should empower them to explore.

And the final reminder: *not all roads start from the homepage.* Our industry has been saying "every page is the homepage" for a while now, and most teams have internalized the importance of brand representation on deeper pages. But have we internalized the need for clear wayfinding at *every* level? When users skip the homepage, or pop into our deepest pages straight from search—perhaps with little to no context for the site they've just landed on—we have to be ready to direct them.

WAYFINDING SIGNALS

In any large or unfamiliar physical space, we have ways of orienting ourselves. We look for entrances and exits. We look for labels on doors, illuminated exit signs, friendly faces. Spaces that care about helping us find our way around will hang maps and arrows and explanatory signage. (Spaces that don't are the Newark airport.)

Online, we can't navigate by the Terminal C Dunkin' Donuts—but we are still looking for signposts to help us along. We might call this *information scent*—a sense of how close we are to the information we seek.

To track information scent online, we look for signals in all sorts of places:

- Navigation structures
- Page titles and headings
- Breadcrumbs
- URLs and other elements in the browser chrome
- Pagination and frames
- Buttons and calls to actions
- Search results
- Imagery and captions
- Text links

Most of us probably don't look for these signals consciously. As our eyes scan a page, trying to spot our sought-after information, we're taking in all these peripheral bits of data (or not!) to build a composite sense of place. Where are we? Where have we come from? Where are we going?

Not that this is existential—we just want what we want from the web. (Hedgehog videos.) And, often, the deeper we get into a site, the harder it becomes to tether ourselves. This is especially tricky if we arrived to a page through search (rather than navigation from the homepage), or if poor site maintenance has left pages with outdated information and broken links.

As stewards of these sites, it's on us to create signals that will helps users understand the space, orient themselves within it, and get where they're going. Three of the most visible wayfinding signals we can employ are breadcrumbs, URLs, and calls to action.

Breadcrumbs

Breadcrumbs are one of the most immediate ways to help users orient themselves within a site. They're textual, but also visual. Done well, they're prominent enough to be spotted by users, but subtle enough not to distract from the page design. They spell out an established path—not necessarily the one the user took, but one that can provide context for where they are (**FIG 5.4**).

Some designers may think breadcrumbs are a waste—that the design should be able to orient users without such on-the-nose details. But even the most intuitive design can benefit from explicit placemaking. Identifying a page's location in the larger system doesn't have anything to do with the strength of the design.

Remember that users are—I mean this in the kindest way—distracted. They skip over information, they forget clues, they misread links (especially in stress cases). Given humans' propensity to miss even obvious signals, why skimp on them?

And if you need even more evidence of their value, SEO-style: yes, Google likes breadcrumbs (http://bkaprt.com/eia/05-01/).

URL structures

URLs are more than an address—like breadcrumbs, they also offer helpfully repetitive signals for understanding a page's relationship to the system.

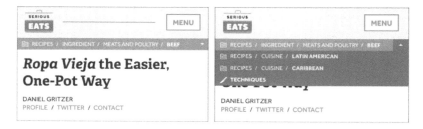

FIG 5.4: The breadcrumbs on seriouseats.com go above and beyond—they show how the recipe is organized in the system (left), while a dropdown offers alternative paths for additional context (right).

For example, what can we learn from a URL like wiltomakes-food.com/recipes/french-macarons/?

- The page is probably titled French Macarons (**FIG 5.5**).
- It is probably organized under a top-level page called Recipes, which would show all recipes on the site.

Most content management systems manage URLs for us, though we can often override them or establish our own strategies. Where we get into trouble is when some of our URLs follow consistent folder paths, and some *don't*. When there is no stated plan for URL structures—naming schemas, subdomain strategies, shortening guidelines—the patterns become patchy and misleading.

URL structures don't just tell people where they are in the site; they also communicate security, reliability, and trustworthiness (http://bkaprt.com/eia/05-02/). This signaling is particularly important in the post-factual era. Many, many, *many* words have been written about the scourge of fake news, but in a *New Yorker* article in early 2017, Emily Nussbaum pointed to URLs, specifically as displayed in Facebook posts, as a key signal:

RECICPES   ARTICLES

WHAT IS THIS?

BAKING

French Macaron Shells

SERVES: 4   ACTIVE TIME: 30 minutes   TOTAL TIME: 1 3/4 hours

Less fuss, minimal muss.

I told you I'd be back once I got the hang of French-style macarons, and now here we are.

First of all, this is *way* easier than the **Italian meringue** method. Second of all, they seem a lot more reliable—though I can't rule out that this is just a matter of my grinding some macaron experience points. I've been going hard on the macarons lately.

"Does it matter if you 'age' your egg whites," revisited:

I tell you, I still have no idea.

FIG 5.5: The URL has *slightly* lied to me about the page title, but not about its location in the system.

> *[Facebook] design made all news-like items feel fungible. On both the left and the right, the advertising imperative was stronger than the ethical one: you had to check the URL for an added ".co" to see if a story was real, and how many people bothered? If some readers thought your story was a joke and others thought it was outrageous, well, all the better. Satire was what got traffic on Saturday night. (http://bkaprt.com/ eia/05-03/)*

Masked or misleading URLs might be good for bots and white supremacists, but for those of us interested in righting the ship, we need to treat URLs as the sources of information that they are. They may not be noticed by every user, but they *are* seen, and they should send the right messages.

Calls to action

Every page should have a next step—a way to continue the journey, an action for the user to take. That action might be submitting a form, making a phone call, reading another article, adding a product to a cart, or sharing a link. It might occur on the page, on a different site, or offline entirely.

The action needs to be clear: users need to know what to do, how to do it, and why to do it. Many pages have multiple calls to action—options for the user, different paths away from the page—but there should always be one primary purpose for a page, and one primary action tied to it.

For example, a product page has the primary purpose of selling me something (**FIG 5.6**). The page might have secondary goals as well—to convince me to trust the brand, to help me understand fit, to let me compare colors—but they are all in support of the one true purpose: convincing me to click that Add to Bag button.

Actions are a kind of navigation, furthering journeys and fulfilling the page's purpose. Pages without actions—without clear purpose—are just dead ends (**FIG 5.7**). They don't offer a direction, provide a next step, clarify information, or assist with wayfinding. Dead ends just...end.

The quick and the dead

Speaking of dead ends: please do not ever create "quick links" (**FIG 5.8**). They go by many different names, but they're the same usability trap if they are:

- a collection of links, with little to no context, description, or explanation,
- arranged as a list in a module or sidebar, particularly on the homepage or landing pages, and
- politically expedient, which is to say, there by stakeholder insistence.

FIG 5.6: This page exists to sell a product, so that particular call to action is the most prominent. Plenty of smaller actions can be taken elsewhere on the page.

FIG 5.7: "Message from the dean" pages are notoriously common to higher-ed websites, and just as notoriously offer users almost no calls to action.

Quick links and their ilk are a perfect storm of unclear categorical criteria, vague labels, and stakeholder arguments—and it all leads to user confusion. As Gerry McGovern wrote on his blog,

If you call something Quick Links, then that surely implies that the other links are Slow Links, doesn't it? I mean, why would anyone choose a slow link when they have the option of choosing a quick link? (http://bkaprt.com/eia/05-04/)

Quick links are the result of poor organization; when content is hard to find, a tidy list of links to expose that content is mighty appealing. They're often championed by stakeholders who feel like their content is being hidden or losing prominence—motivated by fear, not by providing the best user experience.

And while quick links may allay some of that fear, they won't resolve the underlying usability problem. Hidden content can only be surfaced through better structure—clear paths, clear labels, clear wayfinding.

If stakeholders ask for quick links, push back:

- What does *quick* mean? What criteria is being used to choose which links are "quick"?
- Quick for whom? Which audiences are prioritized by elevating certain links (and which audiences are ignored)?
- Why can't the content be found through more traditional routes?
- How might a link list derail or distract from other links?
- How might additional context and more specific labels help users to understand the links?

I'm not suggesting that you can't ever list links. Lists have a place in this world! Just make sure you're creating clear, specific, contextual links because they're the right way to meet a user need—not because there are unsolved findability issues.

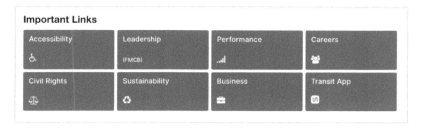

Important Links

Accessibility	Leadership	Performance	Careers
	(FMCB)		
Civil Rights	Sustainability	Business	Transit App

FIG 5.8: I would ask the Massachusetts Bay Transportation Authority why they think only *some* of their links are important, but I don't want to distract them from putting out fires on the Green Line.

WILD GOOSE CHASES

I don't mean to be rude to Harney & Sons, a purveyor of fine teas based out of New England, but I am about to be rude to Harney & Sons, a purveyor of fine teas based out of New England. (It's only because they provide such an excellent lesson on navigation and findability. It's out of love, I swear!)

Now, I like tea. I like it a lot, particularly the caffeinated teas that fuel my workday. I've got an electric kettle and a cast iron pot and a powerful thirst for liquids named for the people and pastorals of the British Isles.

But I don't *know* tea. I am not a connoisseur. When I shop for tea, I know that I want black tea, not green or herbal—but that's the extent of my taxonomic tea knowledge (**FIG 5.9**).

Unfortunately, after selecting Black Tea on the Harney & Sons website, I'm forced to select from a bevy of unfamiliar and inconsistent subcategories of tea (**FIG 5.10**). Even though the subcategories are lightly contextualized with some definitional copy, I still find myself out of my depth, with more tea questions than I started with. *What's a "flavored" black tea? Don't all teas have flavors? Is a "blend" a kind of flavor? Why don't the regional teas count as blends or flavors? Maybe I should stick with coffee.*

For a seasoned tea drinker, I am sure these are stupid questions. But here I am, already using words like "stupid" to

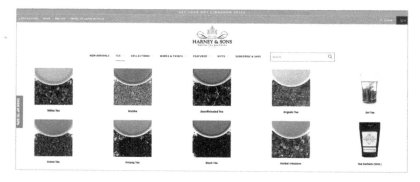

FIG 5.9: The Harney & Sons website organizes tea categorically—White Tea, Matcha, Oolong Tea, etc.—in a dropdown from the main navigation.

describe myself at *step two* in my attempt to buy tea. None of us, including Harney & Sons, want our users to feel stupid.

The only reason I'm in this situation—feeling silly, staring at dried leaves, complaining about the internet—is because I fell in love with Paris. It's a Harney & Sons tea, and after a friend served me a cup, I swore I'd never drink anything else. But, at first, I couldn't find it on the site, because I didn't know how to categorize it. A flavor? A blend? A "tea from other regions"?

They're missing an opportunity to turn me from a casual tea drinker to a knowledgeable brand devotee. This organizational structure cannot help me understand tea, discover new flavors I might like, or feel confident in buying anything other than the one type I happened upon by chance.

The Harney & Sons navigation expects that visitors to the site will already be in possession of two key facts: what tea they want to buy, and how that tea is classified. The site requires specialized knowledge (a.k.a. *jargon*) to navigate—and structural elements like breadcrumbs provide little clarity (**FIG 5.11**).

This is not a system that supports browsing. This system only supports known-item seeking.

NEW ARRIVALS   TEA   COLLECTIONS   WARES & TREATS   FEATURED   GIFTS   SUBSCRIBE & SAVE   [Search   🔍]

BLACK TEA VARIETIES

While black teas are made from the same Camellia sinensis plant as all teas, the oxidation and processing is what distinguishes black teas from the rest. Premium black teas are withered, rolled, oxidized and fired in an oven, creating a warm and toasty flavor. The lengthier oxidation process causes the tea leaves to develop into dark brown and black colors. The flavors can range from malty or smokey to fruity and sweet. Black teas range from mellow teas from China to full-bodied teas from Assam, India. Looking for new teas to try? Check out our tea collections for more.

ALL BLACK TEAS

Black teas are the ones we are most familiar and comfortable with - the teas we drank in our youth. We source only premium black teas from China, and fine tea estates around the world that produce British Legacy Teas. You'll discover many black tea blends to choose from, some flavored and some not. Milk or sugar? That's your choice.

FLAVORED BLACK TEAS

Our flavored teas are some of the most popular teas we carry, at all times of the year. Everyone just loves the way that our smooth flavors meld with the background taste of tea.

ASSAM BLACK TEAS

Assam is India's largest producer of tea, and the broad flood plains make for some of the most fertile tea estates in the world.

BLACK TEA BLENDS

Since 1983 we have worked to create fine tea blends, each one with a story all its own.

CEYLON BLACK TEAS

Ceylon teas can brew up light and bright like Lover's Leap, or substantial like Kenilworth Garden. Ceylons make perfect afternoon teas and can handle milk and sugar.

CHINESE BLACK TEAS

Tea started in China, thus China has a large variety of black teas. From the honey twinge of Golden Monkey and the Panyang teas to the chocolate of Keemuns and the turgid smokiness of Lapsang Souchong, these teas have a range and character all their own.

DARJEELING BLACK TEAS

The light and brisk First Flush teas focus your attention. While the darker teas of the later seasons are more mellow and often have wonderful flavors.

DECAF BLACK TEAS

Relax and enjoy these favorite decaf black teas anytime. Though they've had their caffeine removed, their full flavor remains.

TEAS FROM OTHER REGIONS

Nowadays tea is coming from more than the "Usual Suspects." Please explore these teas from Africa, Indonesia, Southern India and Vietnam.

FIG 5.10: Selecting Black Tea from the Tea menu presents a second level of categorization and a deep sense of existential anxiety.

NEW ARRIVALS   TEA ∨   COLLECTIONS ∨   WARES

HOME / ALL / PARIS

Information-seeking behaviors

The solution to this is *not* to build chatbots and questionnaires. Not to be curmudgeonly, but I don't need my tea-buying experience to be interrupted, personalized, or gamified. I just need the information to be organized for browsing.

To truly understand that, we have to understand how people look for information—that is, how do we search? To borrow from information architect Donna Spencer, there are only a few different modes humans have when they are trying to find something (http://bkaprt.com/eia/05-05/):

- **Known-item seeking.** This is how we search for information when we know what we're trying to find—we just don't know where to find it. Googling an answer to a question, looking up a word in a dictionary, searching Netflix for *Star Trek: Enterprise*, typing "Paris" into the Harney & Sons search box—those are all searches with a specific intent behind them.

- **Exploratory seeking:** On the flip side, there are searches we undertake when we *don't* have a specific intent: looking for a new show to watch, seeing what restaurants are nearby, browsing articles, conducting research. There might be an intention to the search process itself, but not an expected result.

Spencer defines two other search modes, which I classify as more contextualized versions of the first two modes:

- **Re-finding:** When we look for a specific piece of information we have previously found, we are conducting known-item seeking, but with a stronger sense of the destination than before.
- **"Don't know what you need to know":** An exploratory search with even *less* information to start with—not only do we not know what we're looking for, we don't even know what question to ask.

The way people search for information depends on their confidence in what to look for and where they think they'll find the answer (**FIG 5.12**). As web workers, the question we need to keep top of mind is: What must our users already know in order to find what they're looking for?

The challenge with Harney & Sons' navigation is that it assumes the user has the exact same information about tea that the content owners do: it's been designed with the full knowledge of tea on offer as the starting point, rather than the endpoint.

Our organizational choices—through categories, wayfinding signals, navigation structures, and more—are not there to passively move users through a site. They should give users the tools to move *themselves*.

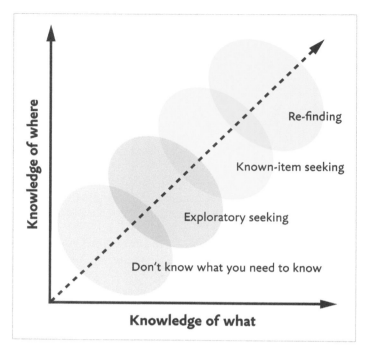

Knowledge of where

Re-finding

Known-item seeking

Exploratory seeking

Don't know what you need to know

Knowledge of what

FIG 5.12: I've mapped Donna Spencer's four modes of information seeking to an extremely non-scientific graph: the more certain we are about what we're looking for and where we might find it, the more specific and intentional our information-seeking becomes.

Findability and SEO

Talking about search behaviors is sure to bring up questions around search engine optimization (SEO). Beyond our structural decisions, how do we know if our content is actually findable? How can we make it more findable? *Whose souls do we need to sell to get to the top of the search rankings?*

I hate talking about SEO because, frankly, it was all quite spoiled by a few bad apples back when Google was a system to game. When some marketers thought the key to findability was to sardine-pack a page with keywords, writers and designers had to expend a lot of energy just trying to make the content readable by *people*. Chris Corak, partner at Onward, an SEO and content design consultancy, acknowledged that this history often makes designers wary of SEO:

> *Sometimes people are scared because they've had an experience of SEO that was just keyword stuffing. But that's not how it's done now. Content should have common terminology, but it doesn't need to be a million times on the page or said in a way that sounds horrible...Often, what the search engine wants is what people want to see, too. Search engines are trying to emulate what they think people like.*

While search is becoming more human-centered, shady practices—clickbait, hashtag abuse, all sorts of weird keyword messes—seem impossible to eradicate. Amazon, I'm talking to you (**FIG 5.13**).

Keyword clutter is annoying. But when that gambit for garnering views shows up in other areas—like, say, the news—it becomes insensitive, corrupt, and dangerous. Take this series of *Newsweek* headlines that appeared after Anthony Bourdain's death in June 2018 (http://bkaprt.com/eia/05-06/):

> *Who is Anthony Bourdain's daughter, Ariane? Celebrity chef found dead at 61*
> *Who is Anthony Bourdain's girlfriend, Asia Argento? Chef found dead at 61*
> *Who is Anthony Bourdain's ex-wife, Ottavia Busia? Chef dead at 61*

In an article for the *Verge*, Bijan Stephen compiled even more examples of *Newsweek*'s insensitive, manipulative headlines, demonstrating that this was not simply an isolated incident, but a purposeful, entrenched strategy at Newsweek Media Group. This could be dismissed as a purely editorial issue—but publishing strategies involve design and development, too, or this dilemma wouldn't be so frustratingly familiar to many web workers:

FIG 5.13: Siiiiiiiiiiiiiiiiiiiiiiigh.

13PCS+7PCS GIFTS

SZKOKUHO 10-20 Pack Puppy Dog
Chew Toys Set Dog Accessories —Plush
Toys,Dog Ropes,Squeaky Toys,Puppy
Chew Toys,Dog Balls,Dog Bone Toy,D...
by SZKOKUHO
☆☆☆☆☆ ˅ 70

$20⁹⁹
Save 5% with coupon
√prime | FREE One-Day. FREE delivery by
Tomorrow, Mar 4 on qualifying orders over
$35

*Every publication has to make this choice: reach for traffic
at the expense of editorial morality or give up that potential
revenue in service of professional ethics. Newsweek has chosen
to take the traffic. (http://bkaprt.com/eia/05-07/)*

I don't know how to fix the publishing industry, but I do
know that this binary—be ethical and lose, or cheat and win—
isn't real. Clickbait and dark patterns don't guarantee traffic.
Chasing short-term wins at the expense of basic human
decency—please, *stop. You're making it worse.*

Depending on your role, you may not have the power to
change headlines—but you do have power in crafting the system, structuring the content, and improving findability. Rebekah
Baggs, partner at Onward, suggested focusing on the relationship between the content's meaning and its presentation:

When you're designing a content module, think about how your design decisions impact the content, as well as how that might impact search. What is this container, and how does it interact with the actual information that will live in it? How are H1s and H2s nested, and how do they appear on the page? If heading tags are treated as aesthetic labels, they won't map to the informational weight that they carry.

Labels and markup have a huge impact on findability—they speak to search robots *and* they assist with human understanding. The goal is for content and design to be in alignment, as content strategist Rick Allen explained:

Ultimately, visual hierarchy has to support information hierarchy. But they are two different things, so if you're not designing with that in mind, there will be a disconnect. Hierarchy and prioritization is what makes information cohesive.

Bottom line: skip the keyword repetition, and focus on the interplay of content and design to help users find what they need.

THE END OF THE RAINBOW

A colleague of mine once worked on a government website where the primary stakeholder insisted that no navigation was necessary on their site—users "only use the search box."

You know, part of me wishes that were true. What a utopia that would be: a place where the only search behavior is known-item seeking, and search systems always parse intent flawlessly, and Nazis have finally been kicked off Twitter. (As long as I'm dreaming.)

Unfortunately, that's not the world we live in. We can't know how our users will navigate our websites any more than we can know what device they'll use to do it. We can only provide signposts to help them on their way.

Still, those signposts count for quite a lot. Navigation structures, wayfinding signals, the content's meaning and design—all of it works together to help users find what they need.

The operative word here is *together*. It isn't just the labels, or just the SEO, or just the calls to action—it's thinking critically, and responsibly, about *all* the signals we send users about the information space. Including the taxonomy.

6 TAGS AND TAXONOMIES

TAXONOMY LITERALLY MEANS "method of arrangement," though you wouldn't know that from indiscriminate use on the internet, where I've seen *taxonomy* refer to a list of hashtags, a CRM database, a sitemap, *a word cloud*. Please stop making word clouds.

The word itself feels abstract—it's cerebral and academic and sounds a little like science? *Suspicious.* Next someone's going to ask us about *engineering ontologies*, and we'll have to nod like we know what that means, and then, listen, I can have my bags packed in ten minutes, it's not too late to start over, there are plenty of countries without extradition agreements—

Okay, okay, let's calm down. We can do this! Sometimes taxonomies *are* very technical, but they can often be as straightforward and approachable as information architect Abby Covert's definition: "Taxonomy is how we arrange things." Holy cats: we've secretly been talking about taxonomies *this whole time*.

For the purposes of this chapter, let's make it even more concrete: a taxonomy is a list of terms used to arrange web content. That definition might not hold in other contexts, but boiling it down to an artifact can help us—and our colleagues and stakeholders—wrap our heads around this sometimes-intimidating idea.

That's not to say there isn't complexity involved! A taxonomy might be "just" a list of words, but that simplicity masks a million different ways those words might interact with your site.

USING TAXONOMIES

First, how do you know if you even need a taxonomy for your website? Ask yourself a few questions:

- Will you have multiple authors and editors publishing and managing content? (And, in the unlikely event that you have only one author or editor, is it possible they will one day take a vacation?)
- Will some portion of the publishing process be automated? Will particular pieces of content be automatically displayed in particular areas of the site, or affiliated with particular topics?
- Will your site's search functionality include any kind of filtering or faceting? Will users control any kind of filtering or faceting as they browse content?

Each of these questions represents a different function of site taxonomy. If you answered yes to any of them (and I know *none of you* can honestly say no to that first one), then you probably need to start on some taxonomic work.

Let's take a look at the differences in those taxonomic functions.

Controlled vocabularies

At its simplest, a taxonomy is just a *controlled vocabulary*—a list of words and their canonical spellings and punctuation, used to help enforce editorial and experiential consistency. It ensures that everyone—your team, your stakeholders, your users—is using the same language and definitions throughout the experience.

You might already use controlled vocabularies in your work, especially around product names or branded terms. Is that department written as *Arts and Sciences* or *Arts & Sciences*? Are news items referred to as *stories* or *articles*? Are your users called *customers*, *members*, or something else entirely?

If this sounds like an editorial issue, that's because it is—or, at least, there's a lot of overlap there. Controlled vocabularies are often found in brand or style guides, ensuring that everyone—from customer teams to the CEO—is on the same page when representing the brand, no matter the context.

If you have a style guide that lists controlled terms, you may be able to use it as a starting point for developing a controlled vocabulary specific to your content. Such a guide can be helpful when creating labels and categories, ensuring that terms are consistent with other user touchpoints.

If you don't have an existing style guide, you can start one: write down your terms, then get input from other team members to make sure the list is accurate and complete. Also write down how the guide will be enforced—that is, socialized, internalized, and tracked in quality control processes—and how terms can be added, removed, or changed in the future.

We may not be talking about a complex taxonomic system, but even a simple list of controlled terms can open up larger discussions about product language, publishing, and editorial control. But the benefit is clear: consistent language contributes to a professional, reliable experience, both for internal teams and end users.

Tagging and sorting

Taxonomies are also used to identify terms—better known as *tags* in this context—that sort content on the site. When specific content needs to dynamically appear in designated areas, we often employ a tagging system to direct it.

For example, when I worked on the website for Carnegie Mellon University's College of Engineering, I mapped its seven key areas of research to seven tagging terms. In order for a story about *robotics* or *artificial intelligence* or *cyberphysical systems* to appear on the respective research page, the story must be tagged

FIG 6.1: This research page for Carnegie Mellon's College of Engineering automatically aggregates content tagged with the appropriate topic.

with *robotics* or *artificial intelligence* or *cyberphysical systems* during the publishing process. Visitors to the given research page can then see thematic articles without having to search, filter the content, or alter the display in any way (FIG 6.1).

Tagging the content in the CMS ensures the page is automatically and accurately populated. But in order for the content author to tag the content correctly during publishing, there must be tags to choose from—the taxonomy.

While the list of research topics for the College of Engineering *is* a controlled vocabulary, its application goes beyond editorial consistency. The taxonomy, in this case, is used to categorize and sort content so that it appears on the correct pages on the site.

The beauty and majesty of tags

Taxonomies are complex beasts, far more elaborate than "just" tags. I have no intention of undercutting their true nature—but for many designers (and users), tags are the most immediate and concrete application of taxonomy.

And they show up *everywhere*. Sometimes they're hidden from the user, serving a backend function that simply funnels the right content to the right places. Other times, they're incorporated visibly into the design, offering users additional topical signals and providing links to related content—like hashtags on social media sites.

Tags, then, are both content and connection. Before it folded, feminist humor website The Toast embodied this perfectly: article tags included topics ("travel"), series names ("two monks inventing things"), and jokes ("opinions I formed when I was 13 with no life experience"), as well as author names. Navigational and categorical metadata were mixed with extensions of the content itself.

As consultant Eileen Webb found when she began working on The Toast's redesign, that mix resulted in an unwieldy taxonomy:

> The Toast had around 4,500 posts sorted into 60 categories. We discovered 8,182 unique tags—6,152 of which were applied only to a single post. More than 400 tags weren't used at all. (http://bkaprt.com/eia/06-01/)

To make the tagging system more functional (for both writers and readers), the tags needed to be audited and sorted—a task that fell to The Toast cofounder Nicole Cliffe. "I am currently going through a spreadsheet with every single tag ever used on The Toast in order to facilitate the redesign," she tweeted in 2015, "and FUCK TAGS."

But the work was worth it. Tags were streamlined into a controlled vocabulary of topics and series names. Categories and bylines were reimagined as new metadata elements in the system, rather than tags. And Webb found a functional way to incorporate the all-too-crucial joke tags:

Women Who Are Dating Peacocks In Western Art History

Women In Western Art History Who Are Pretty Much Finished With Samuel's Whole Deal, Whatever He's Trying To Do

Women Enjoying Heterosexual Kisses In Western Art History

"Oh...No, My Thing Is Happening": Women Leaving Tactfully In Western Art History

FIG 6.2: The Toast's recirculation modules displayed content with the same series or topic tags as the current article.

> *The funny tags (like* truckin' and the continuation thereof*) are a vital and hilarious part of The Toast experience...On the new site, those "tags" are still presented on the front end, but on the backend they're just a plain text field. (The fake tags link out to a Google Search, which we think is hilarious. We're fun at parties.) We kept the funny and the functional, but gave them each their own field so they could be used differently.*

The taxonomic revision worked so well that The Toast's redesign relied almost entirely on tags for navigation. Instead of a main navigation menu, tags and recirculation modules (made possible by the taxonomy) provided almost endless opportunity for users to discover new content (**FIG 6.2**).

The lies and false promises of tags

We might describe The Toast's original tagging system as a *folksonomy*—a sort of free-range taxonomy that's created *through* the publishing process, rather than deliberately designed in advance. Instead of providing content authors with a list of terms to choose from, a folksonomy is created by allowing content authors to add whatever terms they see fit in the moment.

There are benefits to this approach: it's a lot less work up front! And it doesn't lock you into a limited set of terms, which can be helpful if you don't know the range of topics that the content might cover. It also gives enormous creative control and flexibility to content authors.

On the other hand, this system is chaotic neutral, at best. Many folksonomies, sadly, result in a bloated, sprawling, inconsistent taxonomic mess—one that, in the worst cases, can no longer assist in content sorting or findability. Content authors may know their content best, but in systems with weak oversight or sparse content resources, it's far too easy for existing tags to be overlooked, and almost-but-not-quite-identical tags to spring up—to say nothing of typos. In this uncanny terminology valley, articles on, say, professional development may be tagged with *career* and *careers* and *carreer* and *carreers*.

Don't believe me? Go see if there are any Instagram posts under #dogsofinstgram (FIG 6.3). I'll wait.

Whatever work you may have saved up front by avoiding a predetermined list of tags, you've *more* than lost in management down the road. Cleaning up tags is a tedious, thankless task. In the meantime, you've split a single content stream across multiple almost-imperceptibly-different terms, which both undermines your ability to measure content success and potentially prevents users from finding the content they're looking for.

For a service like Instagram, that's not a huge dilemma— the creative, personal nature of the app means that the user is expected to manage their own tags. But for a website that publishes content—and, presumably, wants people to read that content—it's better to establish consistent tags through an enforced taxonomic system.

As with a controlled vocabulary, make sure there's a process for managing the tag list over time. Things change, and the needs of the term list will too: new terms will need to be added, and old terms may need to be retired. Make sure content contributors know how they can propose changes, and that editors or content managers are reviewing the terms regularly. This keeps the tag list manageable and consistent, but still flexible enough for future content needs.

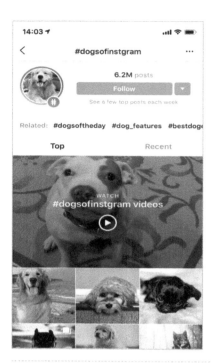

FIG 6.3: Six million extremely good doggos under an extremely misspelled hashtag.

Content filtering

Sometimes we need the taxonomy to go further still: automatically sorting content is nice, but what if the user wants to do the sorting?

When we offer users the opportunity to interact with the content display—through faceted search or filters, for example—we need crystal-clear taxonomies that can be both accurately employed by content authors *and* clearly understood by end users.

We can see this principle in action on Ravelry, a site for knitters, crocheters, and other fiber artists. It's a community, a technical resource, a personal project archive, and a commerce hub all rolled into one. It's deeply beloved by its users—myself included—partially because it fills a need not met anywhere else on the internet, and partially because it's just so thorough:

browse categories

A few of the 200+ categories of patterns... view all categories

Bag   Booties   Cardigan   Cowl   Dishcloth   Dress   Doily   Fingerless
Hat   Jewelry   Mittens   Pet   Pullover   Scarf   Shawl/Wrap   Shrug
Skirt   Slippers   Socks   Softies   Sweater   Top   Vest

FIG 6.4: The basic search, shown here, suggests a few of the over two hundred pattern categories you can browse.

if there's yarn-related data to slice, you can slice it on Ravelry. And, believe me—*there is yarn-related data to slice.*

This is made possible by Ravelry's robust taxonomies, oriented around two cornerstones—patterns and yarns—which each work with a blizzard of data points. Patterns can be classified by craft, by product type (FIG 6.4), by weight of yarn, by needle size, by designer—even criteria as granular as selecting specific techniques for how the heel might be knit in a sock pattern. Yarns are similarly detailed according to their fiber type, color, weight, care, origin, sustainability—the options seem endless.

Faceted search

These extensive taxonomies are set up as separate hierarchies, which then use facets to limit the search results (FIG 6.5). Such granular search leads to precise results—but it only works because of two key factors:

1. The taxonomies have been documented and applied to the system. This level of specificity could never have emerged on its own; it had to be designed.
2. Ravelry users actually *apply* said taxonomies when using the system—and that's what truly makes it sing. The system can only be as good as the users make it.

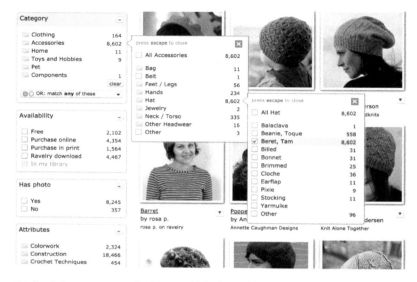

FIG 6.5: Patterns are categorized into multiple, layered hierarchies. Selecting a parent folder—first Accessories, then Hat—causes additional menus to fly out to the right. Depending on the combination of facets, the search can get very granular indeed.

All of the content is user-generated, which means that for the system to work, the users must be willing to fill in the details. Luckily, Ravelry users are a helpful, committed, and detail-oriented lot. The more information they provide about patterns and yarns, the more information becomes available to the community; that information is then automatically pulled in to user projects as useful metadata (**FIG 6.6**).

All of this data makes it easier for users to vet their design choices, explore new techniques, and improve their craft (**FIG 6.7**). Extensive personal notes—about why they liked a yarn, how they modified a pattern, or how they worked through a tricky step—become guiding lights for other knitters. Ravelry, as I said, is as much a record of personal projects as it is a learning community.

About this pattern

Reyna
by Noora Backlund
from Noora Backlund's Ravelry Store

my star rating

☆ ☆ ☆ ☆ ☆

my difficulty rating

▮▮▮▮▮▮

⠿ 10030 projects, in 10208 queues

About this yarn

Pinnacle Sock
by Wild Hare Fiber Studio

Light Fingering
75% Merino, 25% Nylon
460 yards / 100 grams

my star rating

☆ ☆ ☆ ☆ ☆

⠿ 662 projects
📥 stashed 969 times

FIG 6.6: Users can pull pattern and yarn data into their own project records, as I've done here. I don't need to personally track, say, the merino content of my yarn; as soon as I select the yarn name, the system *knows*.

Needles & yarn

Needle	US 5 - 3.75 mm
Yarn	Wild Hare Fiber Studio Pinnacle Sock
Stash 📥	152 yards in stash
How much?	0.67 skeins = 308.2 yards (281.8 meters), 67 grams
Colorway	🟦 Shut Up Wesley
Color family	Gray
Purchased at	StevenBe in Minneapolis, Minnesota
Purchase date	May 22, 2018

FIG 6.7: When I create a new project, I add personal data about the yarn used. The more I fill out, the better it serves as a record of my work, which benefits other users as much as it benefits me.

Trust and community

That community—six million members and counting—has been intrinsic to implementing Ravelry's functionality since the beginning. Jessica and Casey Forbes started developing Ravelry in 2005 when Jessica was looking for a way to connect project notes from different knitters' blogs. They began working on a system that could tag content and standardize terminology—first by identifying terms from Jessica's own experience as a knitter, then by circulating the burgeoning taxonomy with other knitters. The earliest designs netted nearly one hundred responses from other knitting bloggers (http://bkaprt.com/eia/06-02/).

While Ravelry's main navigation hasn't changed much since then, the metadata associated with patterns—and the faceted search that accesses them—has continued to evolve. For instance, in 2010, after making a considerable revision to the pattern metadata, Jessica and Casey asked users to pitch in by updating nearly 170,000 existing patterns in the system (http://bkaprt.com/eia/06-03/). And—talk about dedication—they did.

Such devotion is rare in online communities, and for good reason. Systems oriented around advertisers, systems with poor privacy, systems that protect harassers and punish victims, systems that treat users as data to be scraped, molded, and sold—they do not get to have this kind of community. No amount of taxonomy can save them.

The power of the Ravelry community comes from trust—users trusting leaders to treat them and their data with respect, and leaders trusting users to cocreate the experience alongside them. Carefully constructed taxonomies are the icing on the cake.

DOCUMENTING TAXONOMIES

Now that we understand the different ways we can use taxonomies on our sites, a reasonable next question might be: But how do we *make* them?

Category	Definition	Usage Notes
Topics	High-level descriptions of a piece of content's main subject, purpose, or intended audience.	These terms are primarily for tagging stories, press releases, and events in order to control where those content elements show up across the site.
Departments	All academic departments at Gettysburg.	
Programs of Study	All majors, minors, academic programs, and learning experiences at Gettysburg.	Used to identify academic opportunities to prospective students via the natural language search on the Academics landing page.
Global Study Programs		
Program Keywords	Potential search words used by prospective students in seeking relevant programs of study.	
Publication Types	High-level descriptions of the types of faculty publications and performances.	Publications are drawn from the Cupola's database. Will need to check categorizations against their system. They are used for creating relationships, not tagging.
Event Types	High-level descriptions of the types of events on the calendars.	Events are drawn from 25Live. Will need to check how the types are applied through that system. They are used for creating relationships, not tagging.
Club & Organization Types	High-level descriptions of the categories of student clubs and organizations.	This creates filters for the alphabetical list of all clubs and organizations on campus.
Faculty	All faculty members at Gettysburg.	Faculty names are listed for creating relationships between faculty members and the Course content type. They will not be used for tagging.
Departments & Programs A-Z	The academic programs and departments list that will be displayed on the Departments & Programs landing page.	
Program Divisions	Four administrative divisions for organizing academic programs.	These terms are for controlled vocabulary only. They will not be used for tagging or to create content relationships.
Distinctive Programs	Four Distinctive Programs at Gettysburg.	
Administrative Offices	All administrative offices at Gettysburg.	
Administrative Divisions	Five administrative divisions for organizing offices.	
Clubs & Organizations	All student clubs and organizations.	

≡   Taxonomic Categories │ Topics ▾ │ Departments ▾ │ Programs of Study ▾ │ Academic Interest Search Keywords ▾ │ Keywords by Major/Minor │

FIG 6.8: The first tab of a taxonomy document for Gettysburg College, identifying multiple taxonomic categories along with notes on how and why they should be used.

Remember, a taxonomy is a list of terms—so all we really need to do to begin taxonomy work is to *write some words down.*

Your site probably has multiple taxonomies—perhaps several controlled vocabularies, a tagging system, and a few interconnected faceted term lists. The best tool for collecting all these taxonomies into a manageable system is—you guessed it—a spreadsheet.

I treat the first tab in my spreadsheet as an overview of the system. Because I'm usually preparing my artifacts to share with clients or colleagues who will be acting on the information, I include an explanation of what taxonomies are and how this system will affect the project. Then I identify the different taxonomic categories, with definitions and instructions for use (**FIG 6.8**).

Each taxonomic category identified on the first tab gets its own subsequent tab, where I can build out my list of terms. Sometimes the tab is a simple list (**FIG 6.9**). Other times—such as for tagging or filtering functionality—the list includes multiple associated terms and identifiers (**FIG 6.10**).

FIG 6.9: A basic list of controlled terms: the names of academic departments.

Departments
Africana Studies
Anthropology
Art & Art History
Biology
Chemistry
Civil War Era Studies
Classics
Computer Science
Conservatory of Music
East Asian Studies
Economics
Education

Programs of Study

Search Result	Program Type	Major	Minor	Other Degree
Africana Studies	Degree Program	Major	Minor	
Anthropology	Degree Program	Major	Minor	
Art History	Degree Program	Major	Minor	
Biochemistry & Molecular Biology	Degree Program	Major		
Biology	Degree Program	Major	Minor	
Business	Degree Program		Minor	
Chemistry	Degree Program	Major	Minor	
Cinema & Media Studies	Degree Program	Major	Minor	
Civil War Era Studies	Degree Program		Minor	
Classics	Degree Program	Major	Minor	
Computer Science	Degree Program	Major	Minor	
East Asian Studies Chinese Track	Degree Program	Major	Minor	
East Asian Studies Japanese Track	Degree Program	Major	Minor	
Economics	Degree Program	Major	Minor	
Educational Studies	Degree Program		Minor	
Engineering	Degree Program			Dual Degree
English	Degree Program	Major	Minor	

FIG 6.10: A more complex list of terms: degree program names, along with data about program types and degree options.

You might have three tabs in your spreadsheet; you might have twenty. It all depends on how robust your taxonomic system needs to be to support your content presentation.

As you work, try to collect feedback from everyone the taxonomy will touch—like designers (who need the data for layouts and modules), developers (who need to implement tagging and filtering functionality, or build CMS fields), and copywriters (who need controlled vocabularies). Ultimately, the owners of the content—if they are not you—will need to own this document as well; whoever will be publishing and managing content over time will also be managing these lists of terms.

It's important to note that taxonomies are living documents. They're meant for collaboration and evolution, even after launch. They'll go through plenty of iterations as you work. Be thorough, but don't expect perfection—I've never worked on a taxonomy project where the spreadsheet was ever considered "done."

PRIORITIES AND VALUES

As with any other aspect of categorization and labeling, taxonomies convey a specific perspective. The terms you include, and the relationships those terms create between pieces of content, have a political impact.

This issue came into stark focus when I partnered with design agency Happy Cog to redesign the Gettysburg College website. As part of our strategy for elevating academic opportunities on the new site, we decided to build a specialized search tool just for educational programs. Prospective students could type in any topic they might be interested in—traditional majors like *business* or *physics*, or more divergent terms like *activism* or *outer space*—and the search results would match them to relevant programs of study (**FIG 6.11**).

For this tool to work, however, a comprehensive taxonomy had to relate academic programs to potential keywords (**FIG 6.12**). Some relationships were easy to build: a student interested in art would, obviously, be shown the art program. A student interested in literature would, obviously, be shown the English program.

Or would they? Why would *literature* automatically mean *English* literature? Why not an African studies program or a Chinese language program, both of which include the study of literature?

What about the term *languages*? What would my taxonomy imply if the search results returned English ahead of Arabic? Greek ahead of Spanish? Latin ahead of Japanese?

FIG 6.11: Rather than an alphabetized list of programs (though that's an option as well), the search tool provides a kind of customizable browsing experience for prospective students.

Programs of Study by Keywords					
Topic	Department	Keyword	Priority Program	Additional Programs	
Humanities	English	Screenwriting	Writing	English	Cinema & Media Studies
Humanities	English	Technical Writing	Writing	English	Business
Humanities	English	Writing	Writing	English	
Humanities	History	Civil War History	Civil War Era Studies	History	
Humanities	History	History	History	Civil War Era Studies	Peace & Justice Studies
Humanities	History	American History	History	Civil War Era Studies	English
Humanities	History	European History	History	German Studies	French
Humanities	Humanities	Humanities	English	Anthropology	History
Humanities	Humanities	Liberal Arts	English	Anthropology	History
Humanities	Languages	Arabic	Middle East & Islamic Studi	Classics	
Humanities	Languages	Chinese	East Asian Studies Chinese	Classics	
Humanities	Languages	Foreign Languages	Spanish	German Studies	East Asian Studies Japanes
Humanities	Languages	French	French	Classics	
Humanities	Languages	German	German Studies	Classics	
Humanities	Languages	Greek	Greek	Classics	
Humanities	Languages	Italian	Italian Studies	Classics	
Humanities	Languages	Japanese	East Asian Studies Japanes	Classics	
Humanities	Languages	Languages	Spanish	German Studies	East Asian Studies Japanes
Humanities	Languages	Latin	Latin	Classics	Religious Studies
Humanities	Languages	Linguistics	English	Latin	French
Humanities	Languages	Spanish	Spanish	Latin American, Caribbean,	Classics
Humanities	Philosophy	Ethics	Philosophy	Religious Studies	

FIG 6.12: The taxonomy mapped the school's majors and minors to terms commonly used in American college programs.

What if a student typed in *ethics*? Should search results return a philosophy major? Political science? Religion? And lest we think this is a dilemma only for the humanities: Why *wouldn't* such a term return a computer science program? Was my taxonomy suggesting that ethics aren't relevant to technological disciplines?

The moment we begin building relationships, we begin conferring value. The choices we make about information are derived from our specific worldview—and every worldview is inherently limited. Without actively working against that, we risk doing harm—even with a tool as seemingly innocuous as an academic program search.

The design team and I tried to grapple with these questions. We tried to interrogate our own biases about the programs, the content, and the experience of choosing a college. We created multiple tiers of search results (to better balance relevancy), and randomized display within the tiers, so that a search for *literature*, for example, would never seem to prioritize one culture or language above another.

While we ultimately had to scale back the complexity of the final search tool, my taxonomy work showed me how easy it would have been to make design decisions based on unexamined assumptions—to blindly perpetuate racism, sexism, classism, and other systems of inequality.

No matter how intentional I try to be with my design decisions, I'm still going to make mistakes—and, ultimately, my intentions don't matter. My impact does. Understanding this responsibility is an ongoing process, for all of us.

CONCLUSION

Whatever you're doing, it is not neutral. It is either challenging what's going on or normalizing it.
—JESSICA PRICE (http://bkaprt.com/eia/07-01/)

I wish we could forget Walter Plecker, but, unfortunately, we can't forget the impact of his choices. Among the many dehumanizing outcomes of changing Virginia's racial categories was this: he obliterated the documented identities of thousands of indigenous people. Wiped from government records, they lost the ability to prove who they were—for generations.

Chief William P. Miles of the Pamunkey tribe later described it as "statistical genocide" (http://bkaprt.com/eia/07-02/, PDF). It wasn't until 2018 that Congress passed a law reinstating and recognizing the identities of the first peoples of Virginia (http://bkaprt.com/eia/07-03/).

Let me say that again: Walter Plecker changed a label in 1924, and nearly one hundred years later we needed a federal law to begin repairing the damage.

Information isn't neutral; neither are the choices we make about how to present it, structure it, write it, juxtapose it, or classify it. Every design decision makes an impact; it's just a question of whether we can stand up and own that impact.

That's tough to do if structures like sitemaps and section labels are treated as a matter of course—elements of our work that just *happen* en route to more exciting decisions about art direction or functionality. But information architecture can help us bring more care to our decisions. We can, and should, be deliberate about choices that help people—real people—find, understand, and use information in the world.

The way we organize web content might help someone get a job, pay their bills, write their representatives, connect with a loved one. It might make them feel seen—or feel silenced. It's up to us.

When we organize information, we change it. Let's change it for the better.

ACKNOWLEDGMENTS

First, to my readers: this book couldn't exist without you. Thank you for reading, and for letting me tell ridiculous jokes and get way too enthusiastic about spreadsheets. I truly hope I've been helpful.

To my clients: thank you for all the times you let me organize your websites. And to my colleagues on those projects, especially Kevin Hoffman and Michael Johnson: thank you for your collaboration, wisdom, and support.

To Johanna Bates, Eduardo Ortiz, Samara Strauss, Pam Drouin, Renée Stephen, Aura Seltzer, Rick Allen, Margot Bloomstein, Bekah Baggs, Chris Corak, and Casey Forbes: thank you for sharing your precious time, experience, and insights with me.

To several Slack groups: thank you for the gut checks, panda hugs, righteous anger, friendship, and advice. Here's to learning from our challenges and celebrating our successes together.

To Kristina Halvorson: thank you for giving me so many opportunities to sharpen and share my ideas. Thanks also to Team Confab—y'all are the beautiful beating heart of the content strategy community.

To Donna Lichaw, Eileen Webb, Corey Vilhauer, Amanda Costello, and Sara Wachter-Boettcher: you're the absolute, hands-down, no-nonsense best. Your kindness and smarts have been so instrumental, not just in this book process, but in my life.

To Karen McGrane: thank you for your support, for being so endlessly rad, and for writing my foreword. Your hammer is on the top shelf, but, like, way in the back.

To Katel LeDû: thank you for being such a marvelous editor, boss, cheerleader, and friend. And to the ABA team: what a pleasure to have worked with you on both sides of the publishing equation.

To my parents: thank you for raising me to become someone with enough confidence and grace to write a book. Sorry I used that confidence and grace to put a bad word in the first sentence. I love you.

To Mat Marquis: I'm really glad you're here.

RESOURCES

There is so much information in the world. Confession: half of my bookshelf is utterly unread because smart people keep writing great things and I can't possibly eke out enough time to get to it all. What I *can* do is share a smattering of the books, articles, and tools that were on my mind as I wrote.

History and reference books

- *The Information* by James Gleick is a fascinating nonfiction book about the history of information, offering crucial context for anyone (hint: all of us) working with information.
- *The Discoverers* by Daniel J. Boorstin is another historical tome that chronicles "essential instruments of discovery" like the clock, the compass, and the printing press—in a way, the history of information, again.
- *The Order of Things* by Barbara Ann Kipfer is a reference book cataloguing, well, the orders of things—the temperatures of stars, the hardness of minerals, the values of Scrabble tiles. It's very cool. I'm very cool.

Information architecture books

- *Information Architecture for the World Wide Web* (better known as "the polar bear book") by Lou Rosenfeld and Peter Morville and *Information Architecture: Blueprints for the Web* by Christina Wodtke and Austin Govella are both required reading for anyone learning the discipline.
- *How to Make Sense of Any Mess* by Abby Covert outlines a fun, approachable way to break down information spaces and their challenges.
- *Organising Knowledge* by Patrick Lambe is a clear, useful, detailed look at taxonomy, knowledge management, and business.
- *The Accidental Taxonomist* by Heather Hedden, along with a blog of the same title, offers a *very* in-depth look at indexing, governance processes, and other aspects of enterprise taxonomy work.

Design books

- *Conversational Design* by Erika Hall keeps us grounded in human-centered design practices despite the impending singularity (or, at least, chatbot hype).
- *Writing for Designers* by Scott Kubie is perfect for anyone who doesn't come from a writing background, but needs to get the microcopy and marketing emails done anyway.
- *Design for Real Life* by Eric Meyer and Sara Wachter-Boettcher teaches us to slow down, pay attention, and advocate for stress cases.
- *Technically Wrong* by Sara Wachter-Boettcher is a compelling and necessary read for everyone in (and outside of) the tech industry.

Content strategy books

- *The Elements of Content Strategy* by Erin Kissane lays out the foundations and influences of the discipline.
- *Content Strategy for the Web* by Kristina Halvorson and Melissa Rach is the gold standard for understanding all things content.
- *The Content Strategy Toolkit* by Meghan Casey offers hands-on, practical advice for digital content projects.

Articles about design and ethics

- "Centering the Margins in Outreach" by Marchaé Grair is an excellent lightning talk about designing for anti-oppression (http://bkaprt.com/eia/08-01/; slides, video, and transcript available).
- "You have the right to remain silent" by Dan Hon highlights an increasingly common design pattern that disregards users' agency (http://bkaprt.com/eia/08-02/).
- "Thinking in Triplicate" by Erika Hall asks us to design not for business or even for the user, but for our impact on the world (http://bkaprt.com/eia/08-03/).
- "UX in the Age of Abusability" by Dan Brown is a call to arms to actively consider the negative outcomes of our designs (http://bkaprt.com/eia/08-04/).

Articles and videos about critical thinking

- "Another Lens" is a joint effort from Airbnb and News Deeply to encourage critical thinking and anti-bias discussions in the design process (http://bkaprt.com/eia/08-05/).
- The Critical Thinking Skills Cheatsheet from the Global Digital Citizen Foundation is a downloadable graphic with questions that can be helpful in spurring critical thinking—especially if you apply them to your design choices (http://bkaprt.com/eia/08-06/).
- "The Surrender of Culture to Technology" is a video of a lecture by Neil Postman (http://bkaprt.com/eia/08-07/), though Austin Kleon shared the most crucial takeaways (and related ideas) in a Twitter thread—most notably, seven questions to ask about new technology (http://bkaprt.com/eia/08-08/).

Tools

- Optimal Workshop (http://bkaprt.com/eia/08-09/) is a remote usability testing suite. I particularly love the Treejack tool, which I use for testing sitemap concepts—a great way to collect user feedback on labels and hierarchies.
- The Content Analysis Tool (CAT) from Content Insight is a straightforward, easy-to-use automated auditing tool, perfect for baseline data and analytics (http://bkaprt.com/eia/08-10/).
- Screaming Frog (http://bkaprt.com/eia/08-11/) and URL Profiler (http://bkaprt.com/eia/08-12/) are automated audit tools; I run the crawl with the former, then feed the results into the latter, which generates a very robust (sometimes unwieldy) spreadsheet.
- Boardthing is like digital sticky notes; I use it for plotting sitemaps, organizing user feedback, and other tasks that make more sense when visualized as small colorful rectangles (http://bkaprt.com/eia/08-13/).

Also, read more poetry. It might not make you better at organizing websites, but it will make you happy.

REFERENCES

Shortened URLs are numbered sequentially; the related long URLs are listed below for reference.

Introduction

00-01   https://www.encyclopediavirginia.org/Plecker_Walter_Ashby_1861-1947

Chapter 1

01-01   http://www.startribune.com/display-your-books-by-color-shape-i-don-t-care-just-don-t-turn-them-spine-in/480987341/

01-02   https://techcrunch.com/2018/09/17/twitter-chronological-timeline/

01-03   https://www.whats-on-netflix.com/library/categories/

01-04   http://www.isisinform.com/unlatched-richard-saul-wurman%E2%80%99s-theory-of-limitations/

Chapter 2

02-01   https://jarango.com/2018/12/28/designing-a-better-system/

02-02   http://thefutureislikepie.com/pivot-tables-are-magic/

Chapter 3

03-01   http://mcmansionhell.com/post/171906495491/looking-around-all-buildings-are-interesting

03-02   https://www.nngroup.com/articles/audience-based-navigation/

03-03   https://www.linkedin.com/pulse/benefits-single-task-driven-classification-navigation-gerry-mcgovern

03-04   http://gerrymcgovern.com/organize-around-the-customer-task/

03-05   https://www.thinkcompany.com/2018/03/the-revolution-will-have-structured-content/

03-06   https://en.wikipedia.org/wiki/Wastebasket_taxon

03-07   https://twitter.com/Documentalope/status/930808114319835136

Chapter 4

04-01 http://bkaprt.com/resources/everyday-information-architecture/Structural_Audit_Sheet.xlsx

Chapter 5

05-01 https://twitter.com/methode/status/877842242358185984

05-02 https://www.wordfence.com/blog/2017/01/gmail-phishing-data-uri/

05-03 http://www.newyorker.com/magazine/2017/01/23/how-jokes-won-the-election

05-04 http://gerrymcgovern.com/quick-links-slow-links-and-bad-navigation-design/

05-05 http://boxesandarrows.com/four-modes-of-seeking-information-and-how-to-design-for-them/

05-06 https://twitter.com/ashleyfeinberg/status/1005078127289290754

05-07 https://www.theverge.com/2018/6/12/17448816/newsweek-anthony-bourdain-seo-headlines-suicide-contagion

Chapter 6

06-01 https://responsivewebdesign.com/toast/taxonomy/

06-02 http://www.frecklegirl.com/blog/2005/04/12/knitters-help/

06-03 http://blog.ravelry.com/2010/07/09/its-time-for-a-ravelry-search-party/

Conclusion

07-01 https://twitter.com/Delafina777/status/903646892801667072

07-02 https://www.nps.gov/jame/learn/historyculture/upload/Documentary-Genocide.pdf

07-03 https://www.congress.gov/bill/115th-congress/house-bill/984

Resources

08-01 https://www.confabevents.com/videos/confab-2018-lightning-talks

08-02 https://medium.com/@hondanhon/you-have-the-right-to-remain-silent-6c5df21db27f

08-03 https://medium.com/mule-design/a-three-part-plan-to-save-the-world-98653a20a12f

08-04 https://greenonions.com/ux-in-the-age-of-abusability-797cd01f6b13

08-05 https://airbnb.design/anotherlens/

08-06 https://globaldigitalcitizen.org/critical-thinking-skills-cheat-sheet-infographic

08-07 https://www.youtube.com/watch?v=hlrv7DIHlIE

08-08 https://twitter.com/austinkleon/status/831190932255031300

08-09 https://www.optimalworkshop.com/

08-10 https://www.content-insight.com/products

08-11 https://www.screamingfrog.co.uk/

08-12 https://urlprofiler.com/

08-13 https://boardthing.com/

INDEX

A

Allen, Rick 97
Arango, Jorge 20
audits 19-22
    audit definitions 20-24
    automated data 29
    determining scope 23
    parsing data 32
    resource planning 27-28
    structural audit template (down-
        load) 62
    structure (auditing for) 57-64

B

Baggs, Rebekah 96
Barrett, Sarah R. 55
Bertolucci, Katherine 16

C

categorization
    business goals 41-42
    current state 42-43
    future state 44-46
    user needs 39-40
Cliffe, Nicole 103
CMS 26
content audit, definition 20
content inventory 20, 29
Conway's Law 42
Corak, Chris 95
Covert, Abby 99
Criteria Matching 37-38

F

folksonomy 104-105
Forbes, Jessica and Casey 110

G

grouping 16

H

Hall, Erika 54
Hertzel, Laurie 4

I

information scent 82
information-seeking 89-97

K

Kipfer, Barbara Ann 4
Kissane, Erin 63

L

labeling
    guidelines 51-54
    language versus criteria 48-50
    microcopy 51

M

McGovern, Gerry 40, 88
Miles, Chief William P. (of the
        Pamunkey tribe) 116

N

navigation structures 77-78
navigation & wayfinding
    breadcrumbs 83
    calls to action 86-87
    pathways 81-82
    quick links 86
    URL structures 83-86
Nussbaum, Emily 84-85

O

ordering 16
organization frameworks 5
    LATCH (Location, Alphabet, Time,
        Category, Heirarchy) 5-13

P

Plecker, Walter 1, 116
Price, Jessica 116

S

SEO 83, 94-97
sitemaps 65-72
    documentation styles 67-71
    iterating 72-73
Spencer, Donna 92-93
Stephen, Bijan 95

T

taxonomies 100-109
    content filtering 106-110
    controlled vocabularies 100-101
    documentation 110-112
    tagging and sorting 101-106
Thomas, Dave 48

W

wayfinding signals 82-89
Wurman, Richard Saul 2, 12

ABOUT A BOOK APART

We cover the emerging and essential topics in web design and development with style, clarity, and above all, brevity—because working designer-developers can't afford to waste time.

COLOPHON

The text is set in FF Yoga and its companion, FF Yoga Sans, both by Xavier Dupré. Headlines and cover are set in Titling Gothic by David Berlow.

 This book was printed in the United States using FSC certified papers.

FSC
www.fsc.org

ABOUT THE AUTHOR

Lisa Maria Martin is an independent consultant based in Boston. She practices content-driven information architecture, helping organizations to understand, organize, and structure their web content for empowering user experiences. She is the managing editor of A Book Apart, as well as a writer, speaker, workshop facilitator, and poet. Learn more about her approach at thefutureislikepie.com.